[509] Snow City
Lac Lioson CH

[463]　　Reclaim after Reclaim
　　　　Manama BH

↓P162

[269] Material Gesture
NL, BE
↓P150

[456] Reclaim after Reclaim
Manama BH
↓P162

[271] Material Gesture
NL, BE

↓P150

[262] Zoomscape
Fabulous Future, Amsterdam NL
↓P168

[530] The Suburban Voyage
Rotterdam NL

[172]   In Progress
        Sao Miguel, Azores PT

↓P144

[494] Self Built Universes
       Lisbon PT
       ↓P162

[258]   Lesbos Falafel
        Mytilini, Lesbos GR

[364] No Borders
La Jungle, Calais FR

↓P156

[503]   Self Built Universes
        Lisbon PT

↓P162

[414] Palermo Appendix
Manifesta, Palermo IT

[573]   Testing the Frontline
        Nieuw West, The Bijlmer and Vogelbuurt, Amsterdam NL

[283] Nagele by Nagele
Nagele NL
20 ↓P150

[363] No Borders
La Jungle, Calais FR
↓P156

[469]　Reclaim after Reclaim
　　　　Manama BH

↓P162

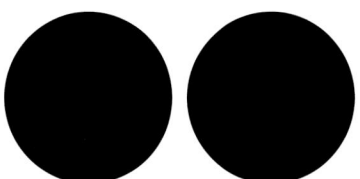

[263] Material Gesture
NL, BE

[571] Testing the Frontline
       Nieuw-West, The Bijlmer and Vogelenbuurt, Amsterdam NL

28   ↓P166

[454] Reclaim after Reclaim
Manama BH

↓P162

[161]   In Progress
        Sao Miguel, Azores PT
        ↓P144

[274]　Material Gesture
　　　　NL, BE

↓P150

[124]   Green Light
        Amsterdam NL
↓ P142

[532] The Suburban Voyage
       Rotterdam NL

↓ P164

[179] In Progress
       Sao Miguel, Azores PT

↓P144   35

[447] Port Nord
Port Nord, Chalon-sur-Saône FR
↓P160

[422] Palermo Appendix
Manifesta, Palermo IT
↓P158

[537]   The Suburban Voyage
        Rotterdam NL
↓ P164

[533]　　The Suburban Voyage
　　　　Rotterdam NL

[429]　Pick-Up
　　　　Butchers Tears, Amsterdam NL

42　↓P160

[561]　Tabula Rasa
　　　　Amsterdam NL

↓P166

[450]　Port Nord
　　　　Port Nord, Chalon-sur-Saône FR
↓P160

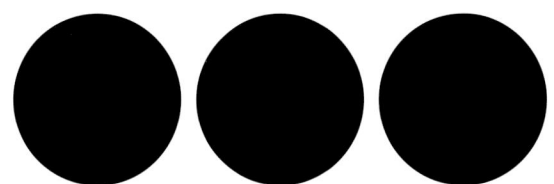

[538]   Table of Content
        De Fabriek, Eindhoven NL

[367] No Borders
       La Jungle, Calais FR

↓P156

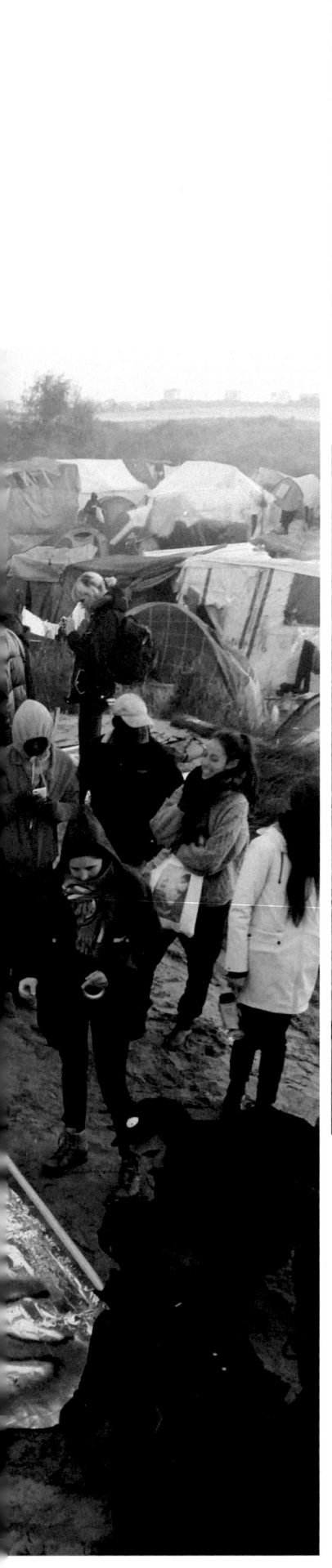

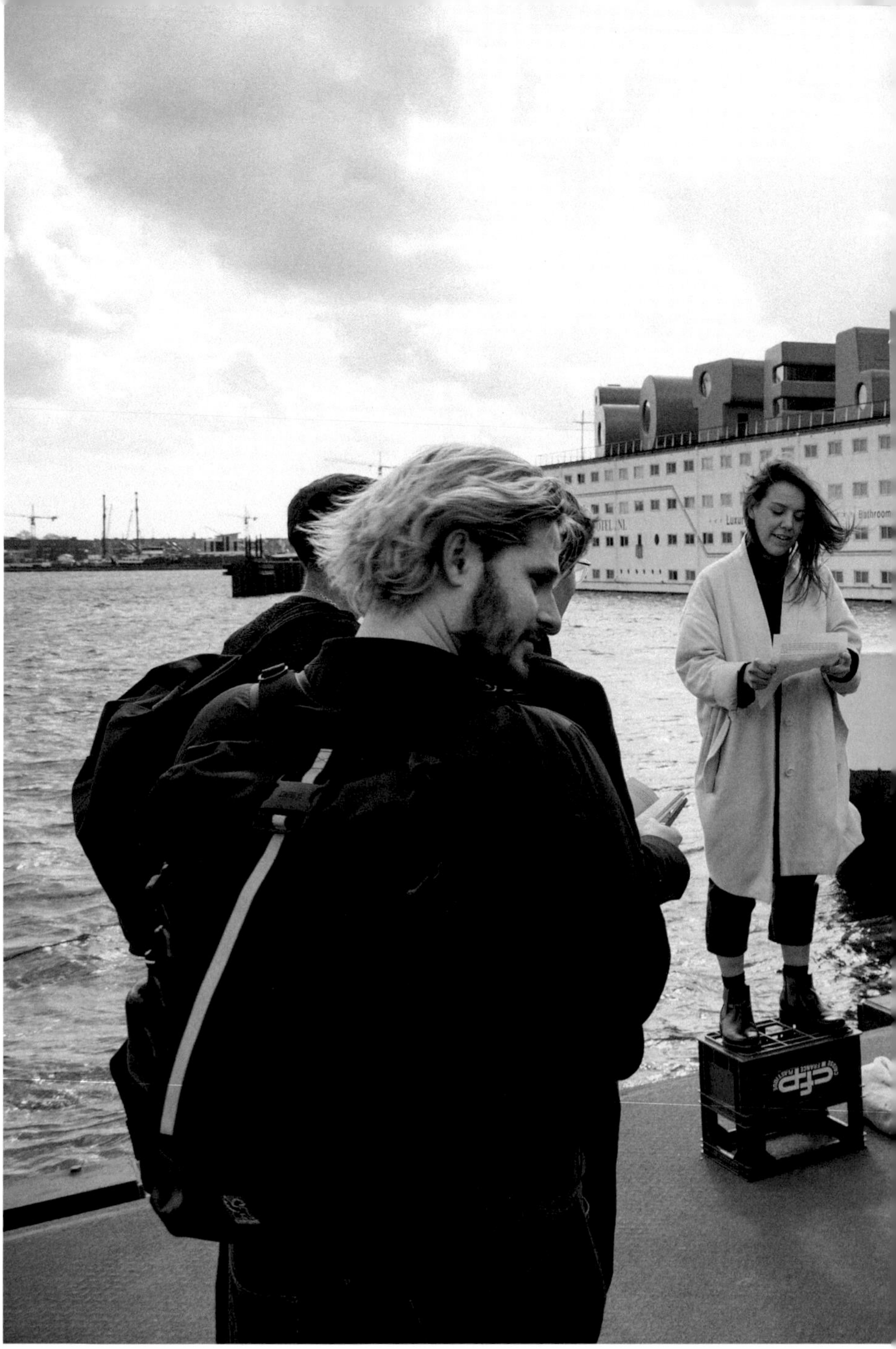

[044] Boarding Ticket
Ferry Terminal direction NDSM, Central Station, Amsterdam NL

↓P136

[254] Jojo's Bizare Adventure
       Kas Keerweer, Amsterdam NL

[541]   Table of Content
        De Fabriek, Eindhoven NL
 ↓P164

[281] Nagele by Nagele
       Nagele NL

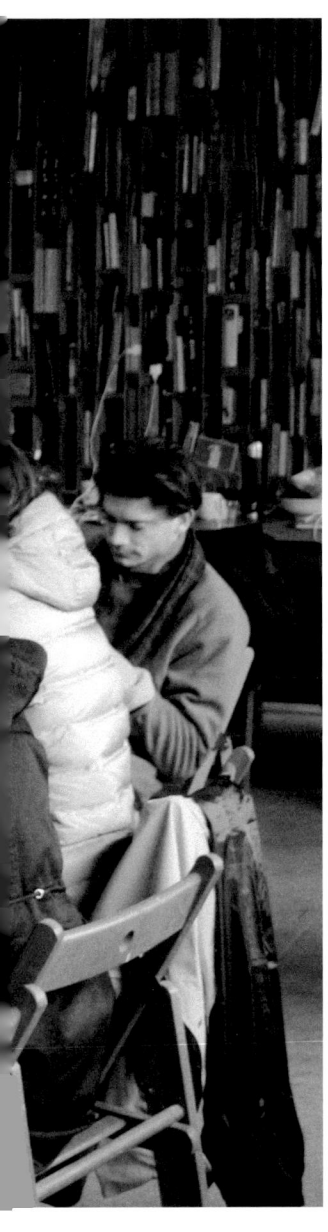

[600]　　The Wild Beyond
　　　　　Amsterdam NL

↓ P168

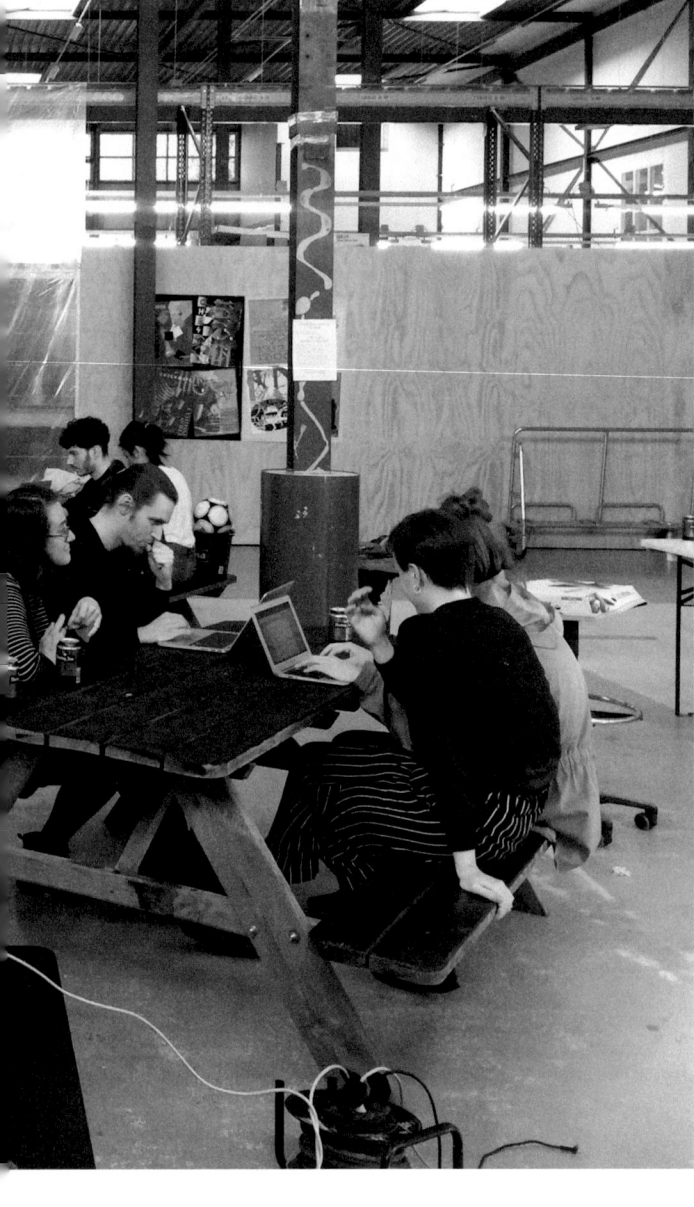

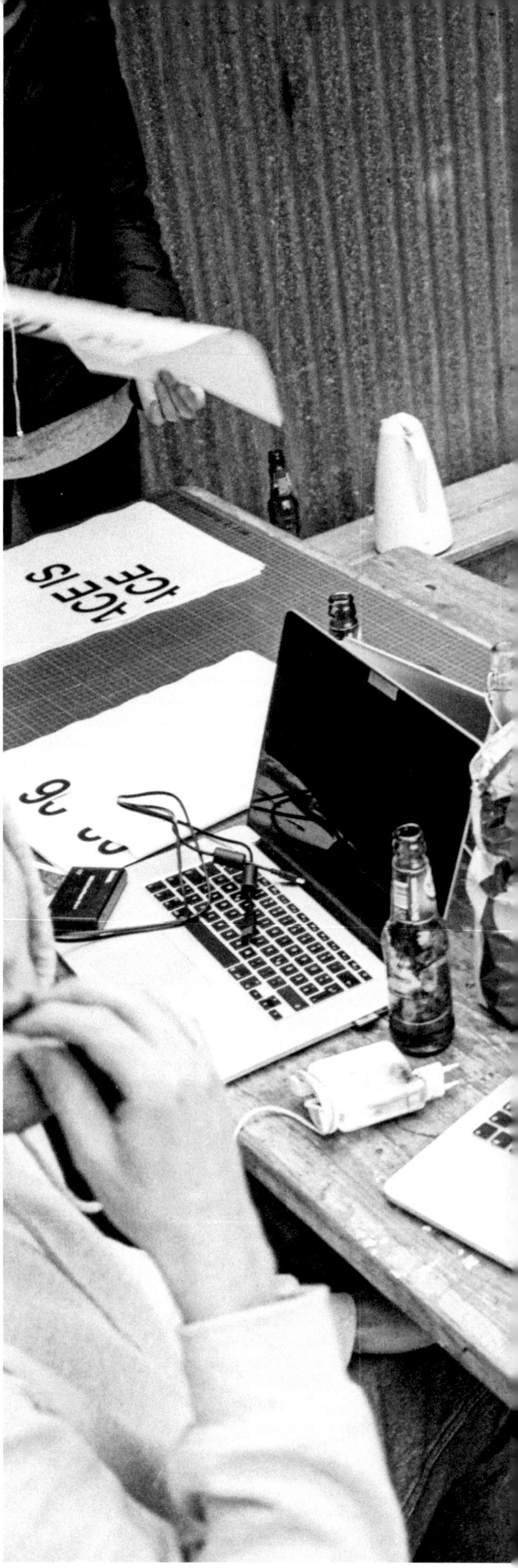

[540] Table of Content
De Fabriek, Eindhoven NL

↓P164

[237] Instant Composition
       Extra City, Antwerpen BE
↓P148

[451]   Port Nord
        Port Nord, Chalon-sur-Saône FR
        ↓P160

[549]   Tabula Rasa
        Amsterdam NL

[529]   The Suburban Voyage
         Rotterdam NL

[194]   In the Open
        Van Ostadestraat, Amsterdam NL
        ↓ P146

[356]   No Borders
        La Jungle, Calais FR

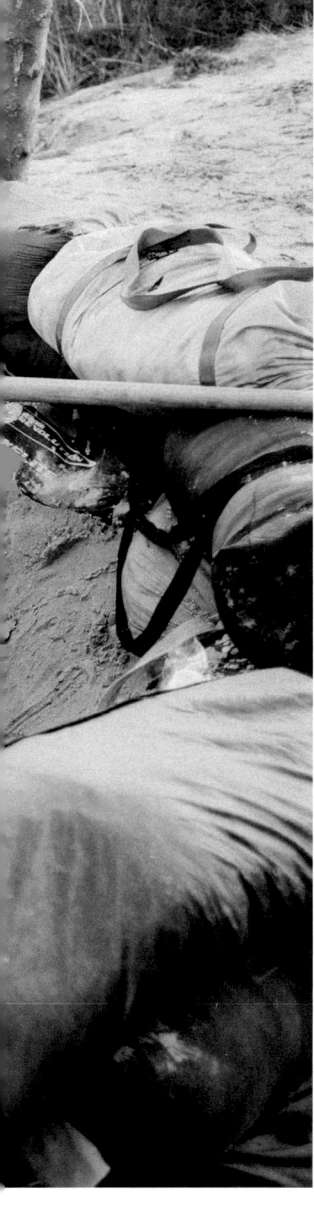

[512] Snow City
       Lac Lioson CH

↓P164

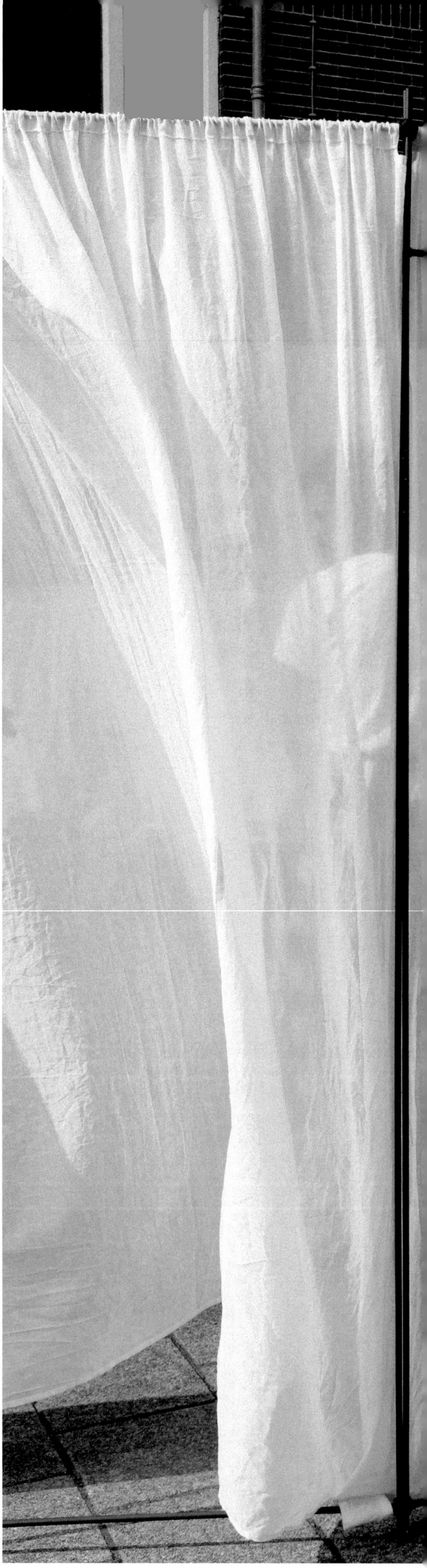

[201] In the Open
       Van Ostadestraat, Amsterdam NL
       ↓P146

[309] New Town
Station Noord, Amsterdam NL

↓P152

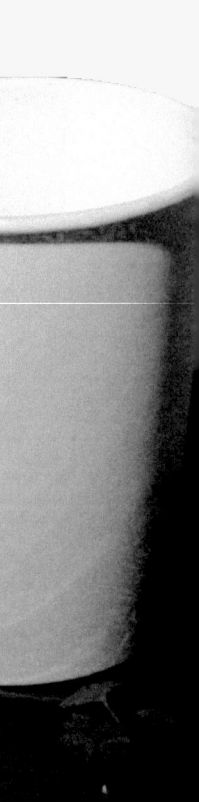

[001]   Alumni Event
        Sandberg Instituut, Amsterdam NL
↓P136

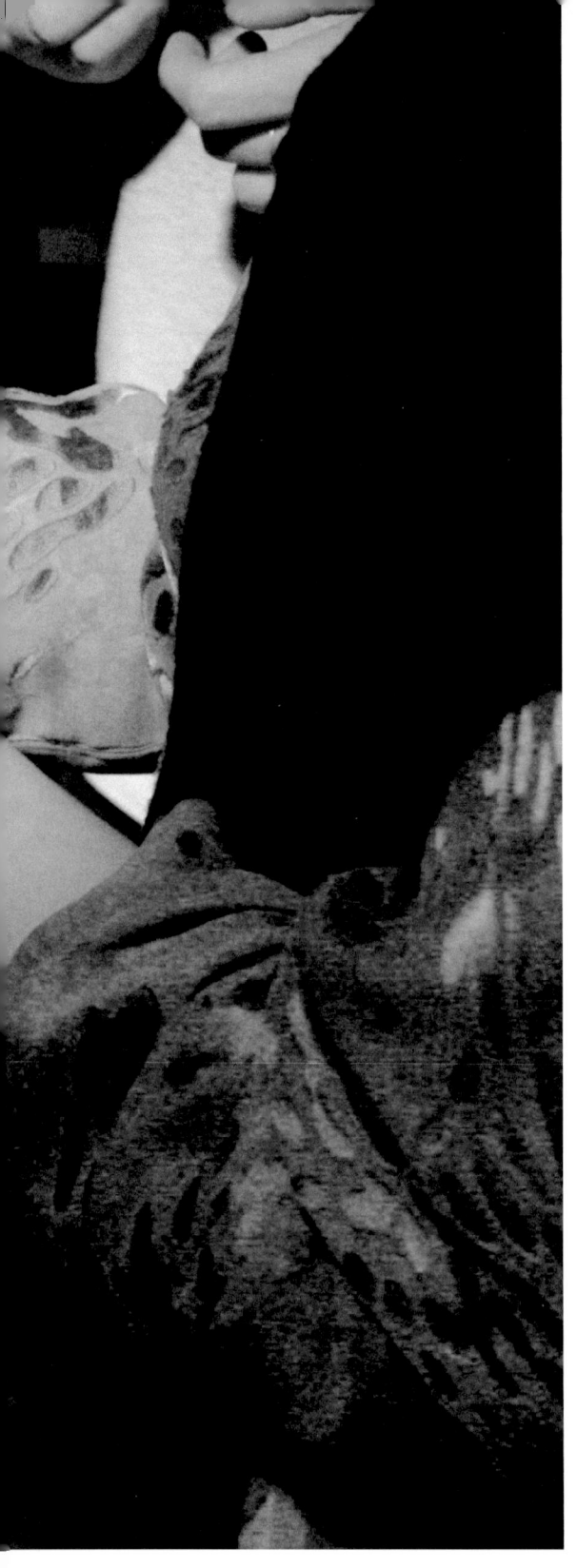

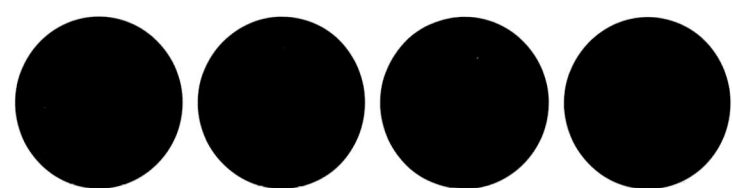

[347] No Borders
La Jungle, Calais FR

[268] Material Gesture
NL, BE

↓P150

[147] The House
       Schipol NL

↓P144

[262] Material Gesture
NL, BE
↓P150

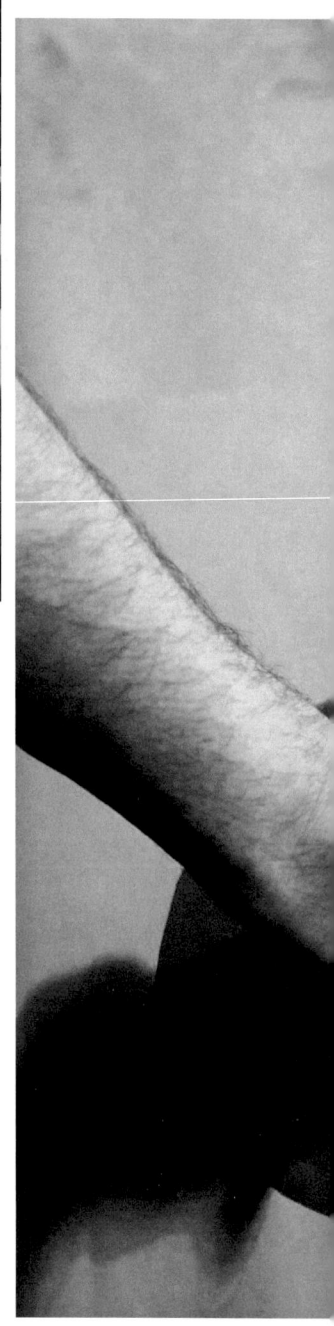

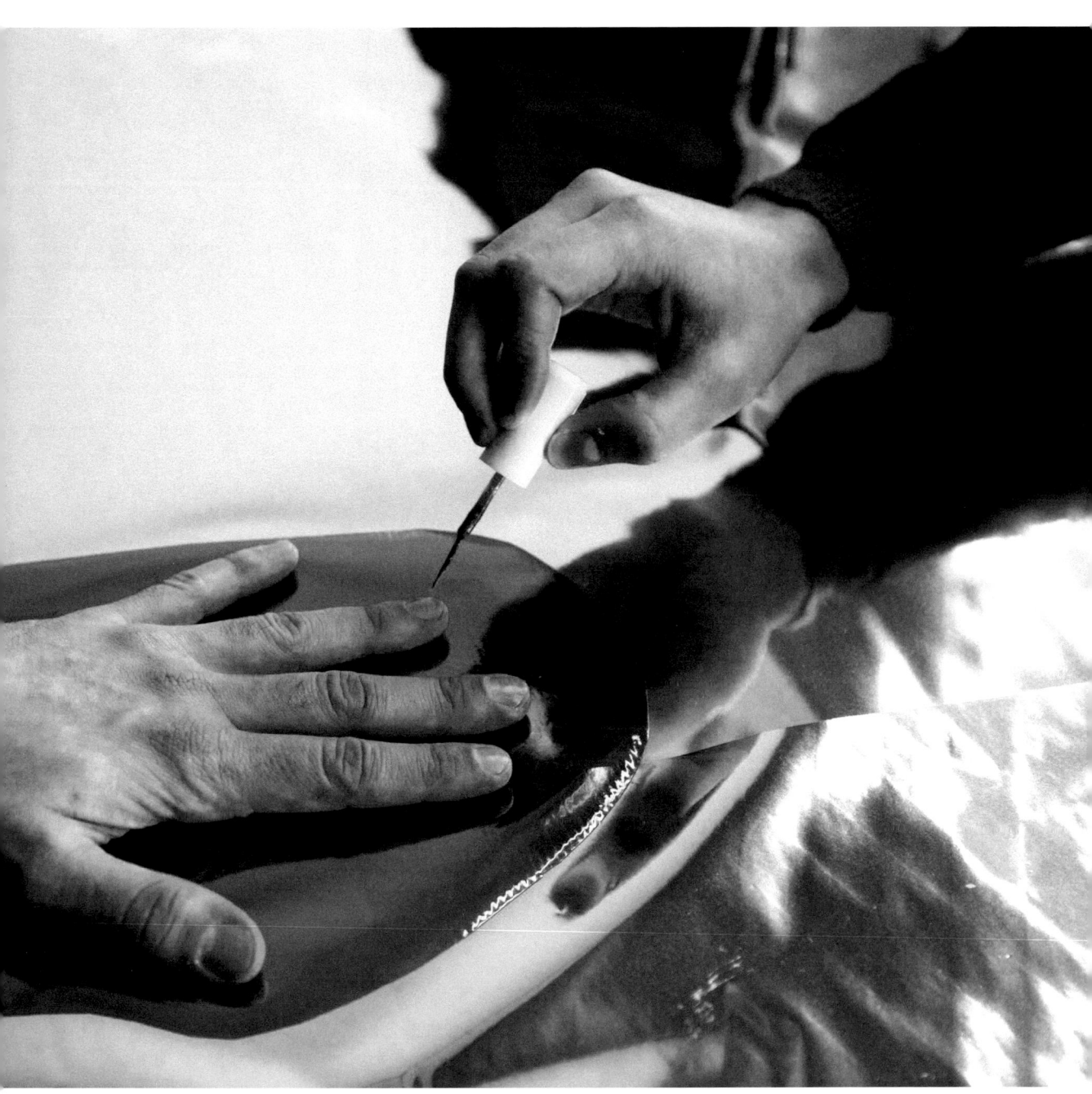

[594] Unequal Club
DeSchool Club, Amsterdam NL
↓P168

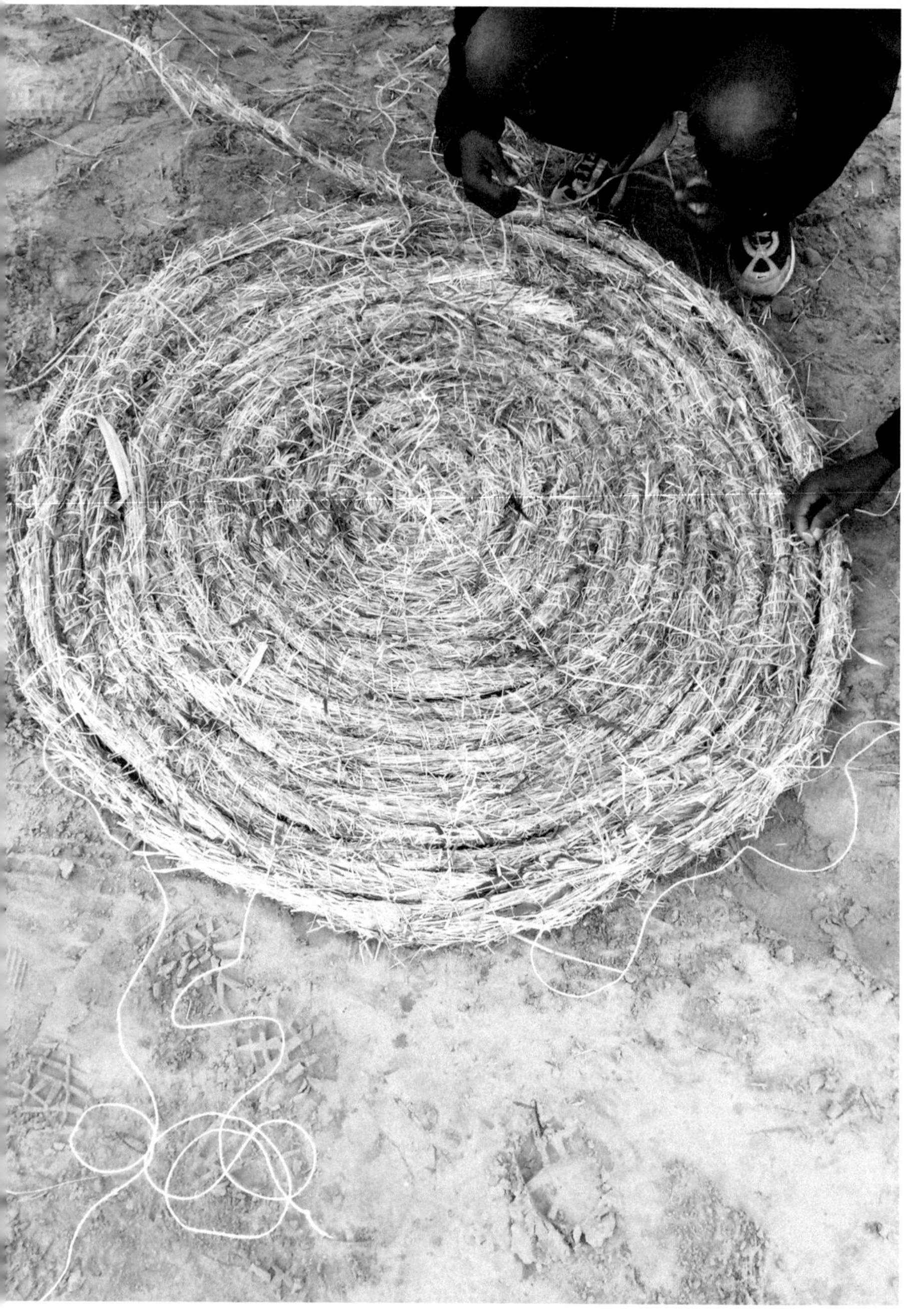

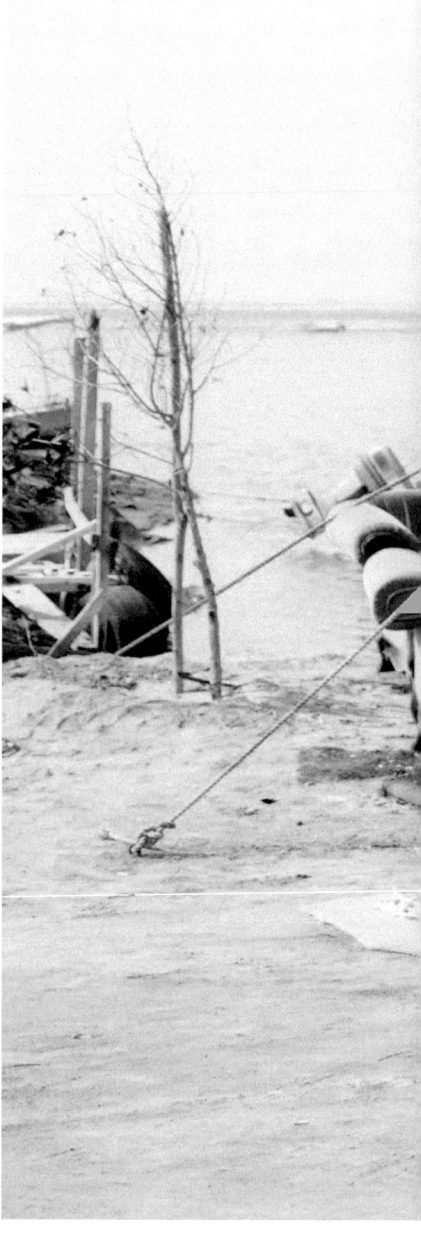

[355] No Borders
La Jungle, Calais FR

[478] Reclaim after Reclaim
Manama BH

↓P156

↓P162

[080]　Critical Studio
　　　　Sandberg Instituut, Amsterdam NL
　　　　↓P138

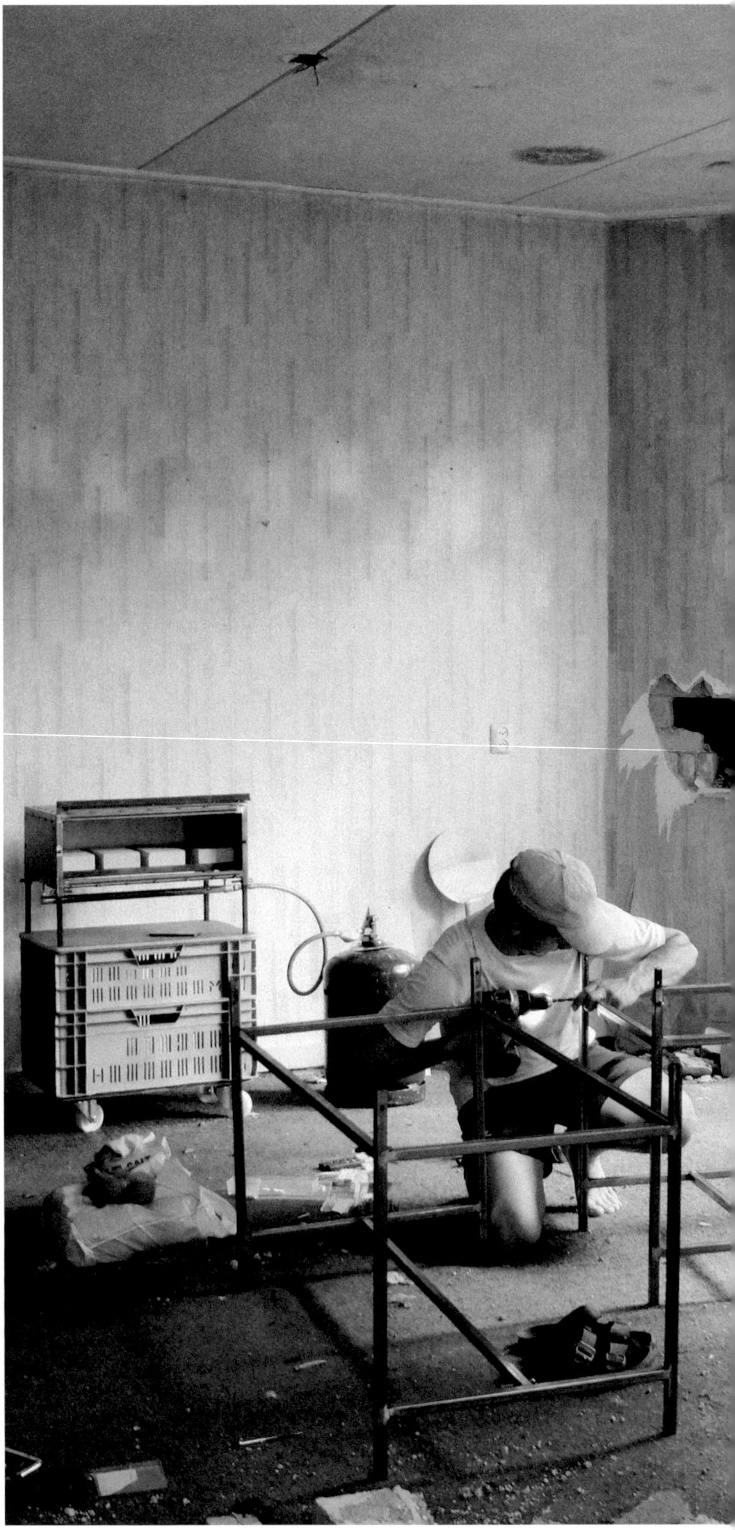

[539] Table of Content
       De Fabriek, Eindhoven NL
       ↓P164

[135] The House
       Schipol NL
       ↓P144

[FF04]   Fabulous Future
         Amsterdam NL
↓P142   81

[501] Self Built Universes
       Lisbon PT
       ↓P162

[360] No Borders
       La Jungle, Calais FR
↓P156

[516] Snow City
Lac Lioson CH

↓P164

[351] No Borders
La Jungle, Calais FR
↓P156

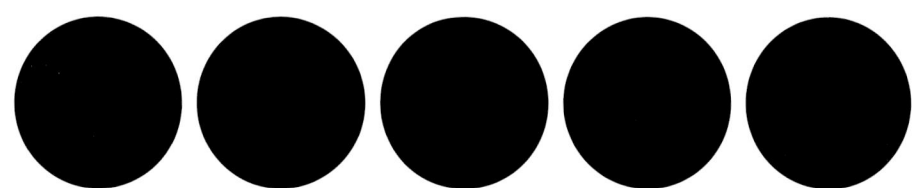

[108] ■ The Garden of (Un)/Becoming Malissa Anne Canez Sabus ↓P140

[060] ■ Case Study Contribution Francesca Lucchitta ↓P138

[337] Dig: Positive Bodies
Kim Wawer

↓P154

[238] Jam Contribution
Giedre Lisauskaite

↓P148

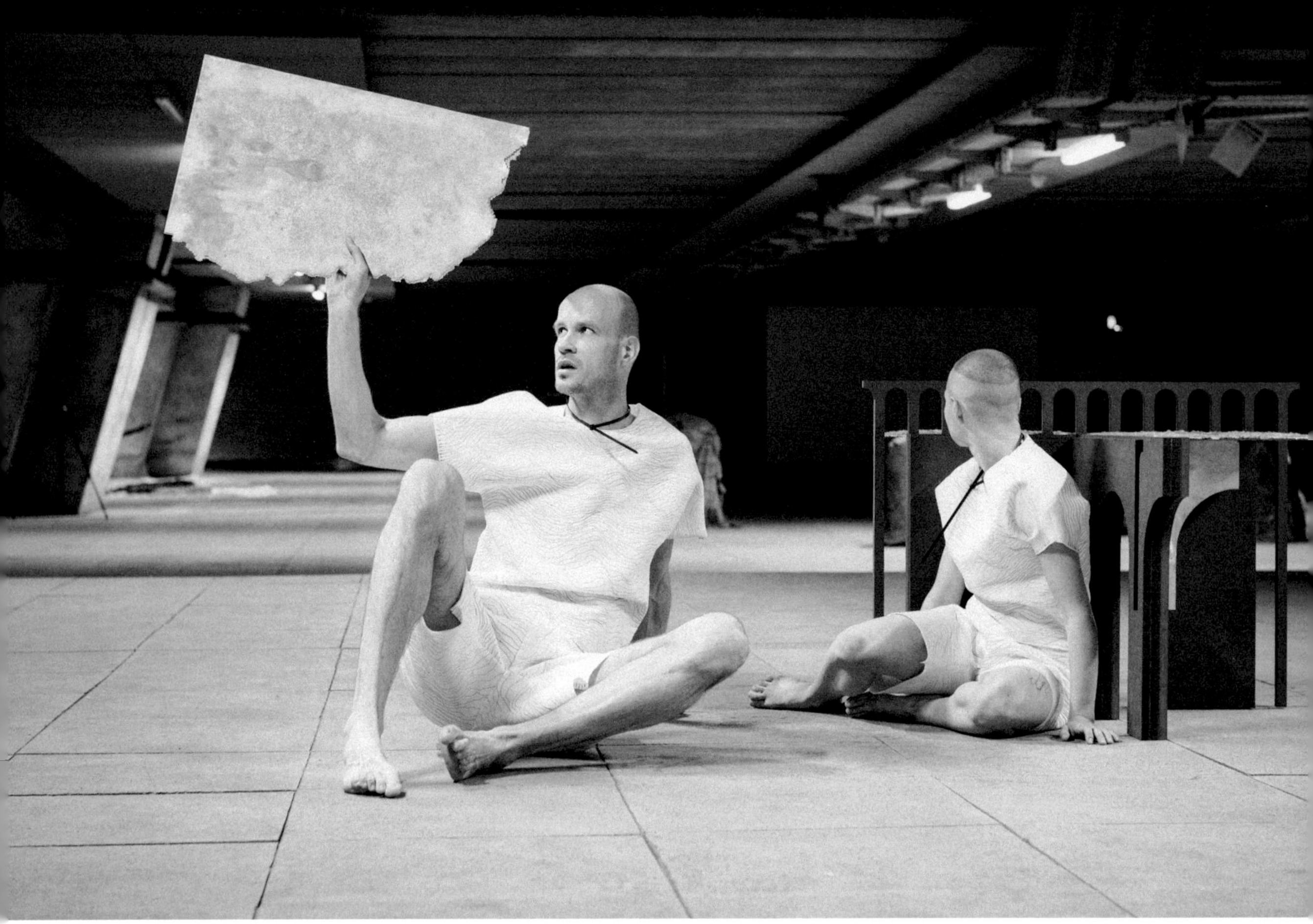

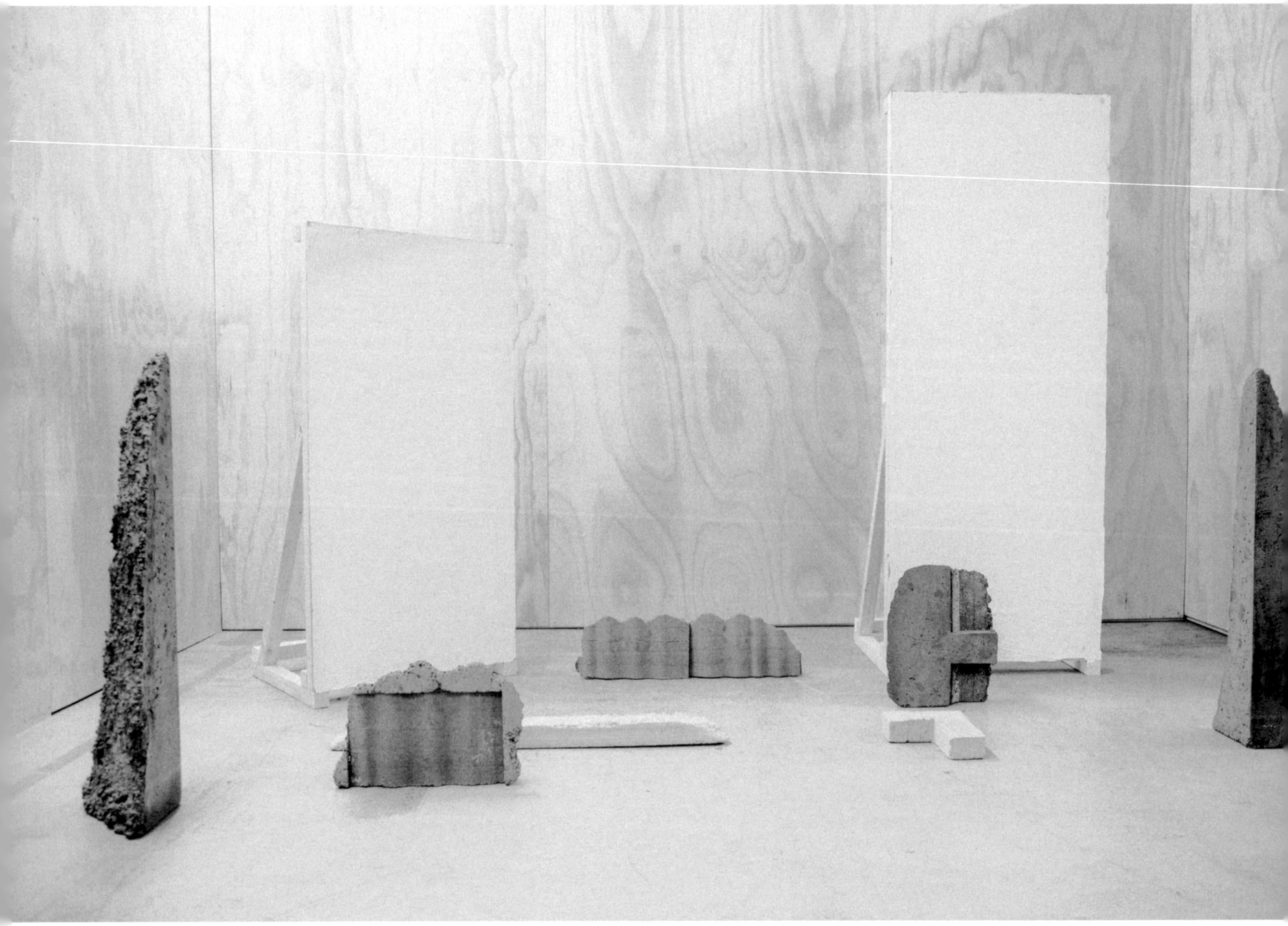

[296] ▀ DMM
Arie de Fijter

[indv] ▄ Emoticons
Samuel Kuhfuss Gustavsen

↓P152

[219] ■ Secure, Peaceful & Wild
Mathilde Stubmark
↓P146

[544] ■ Tabula Rasa Contribution
Elia Castino
↓P166

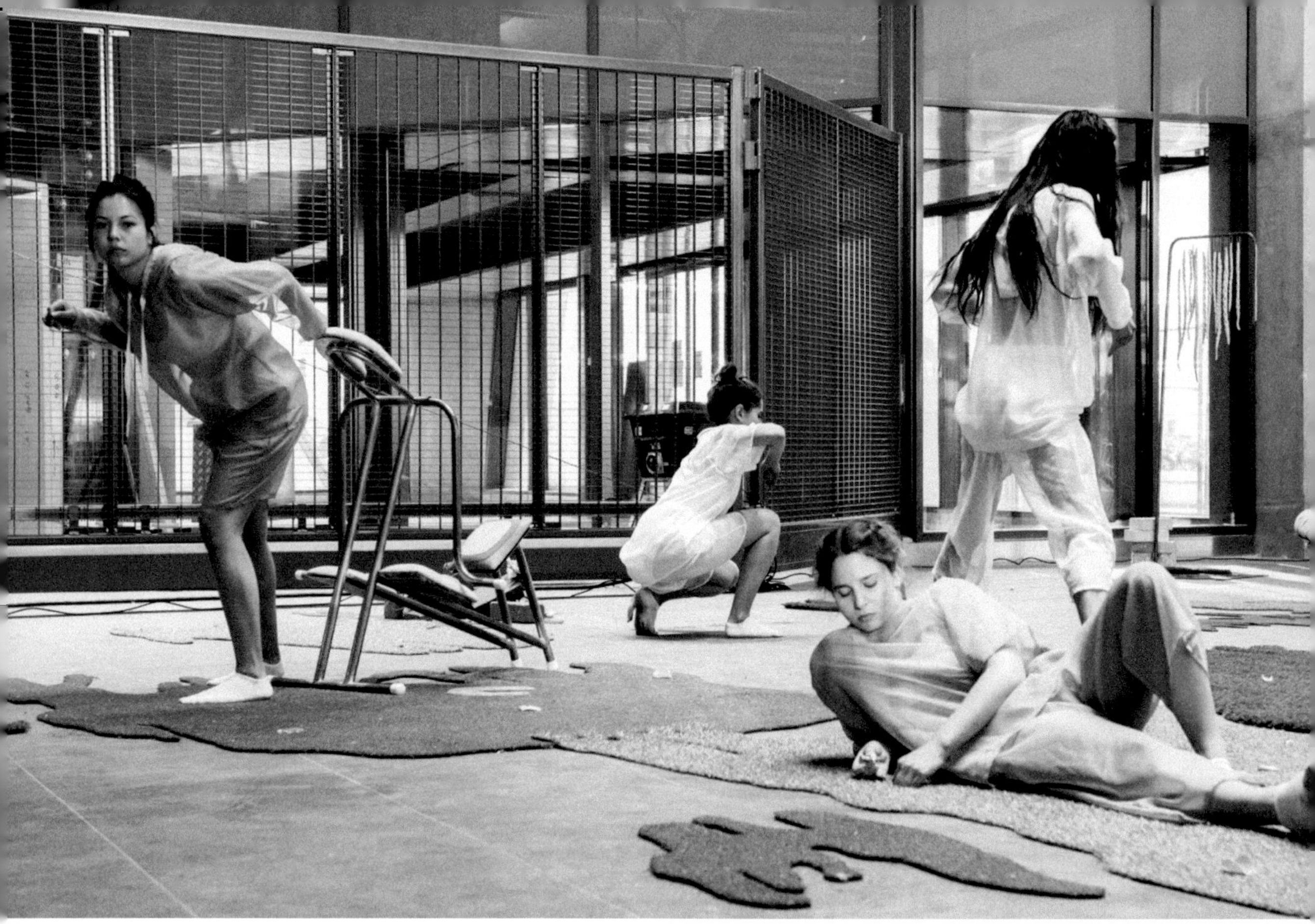

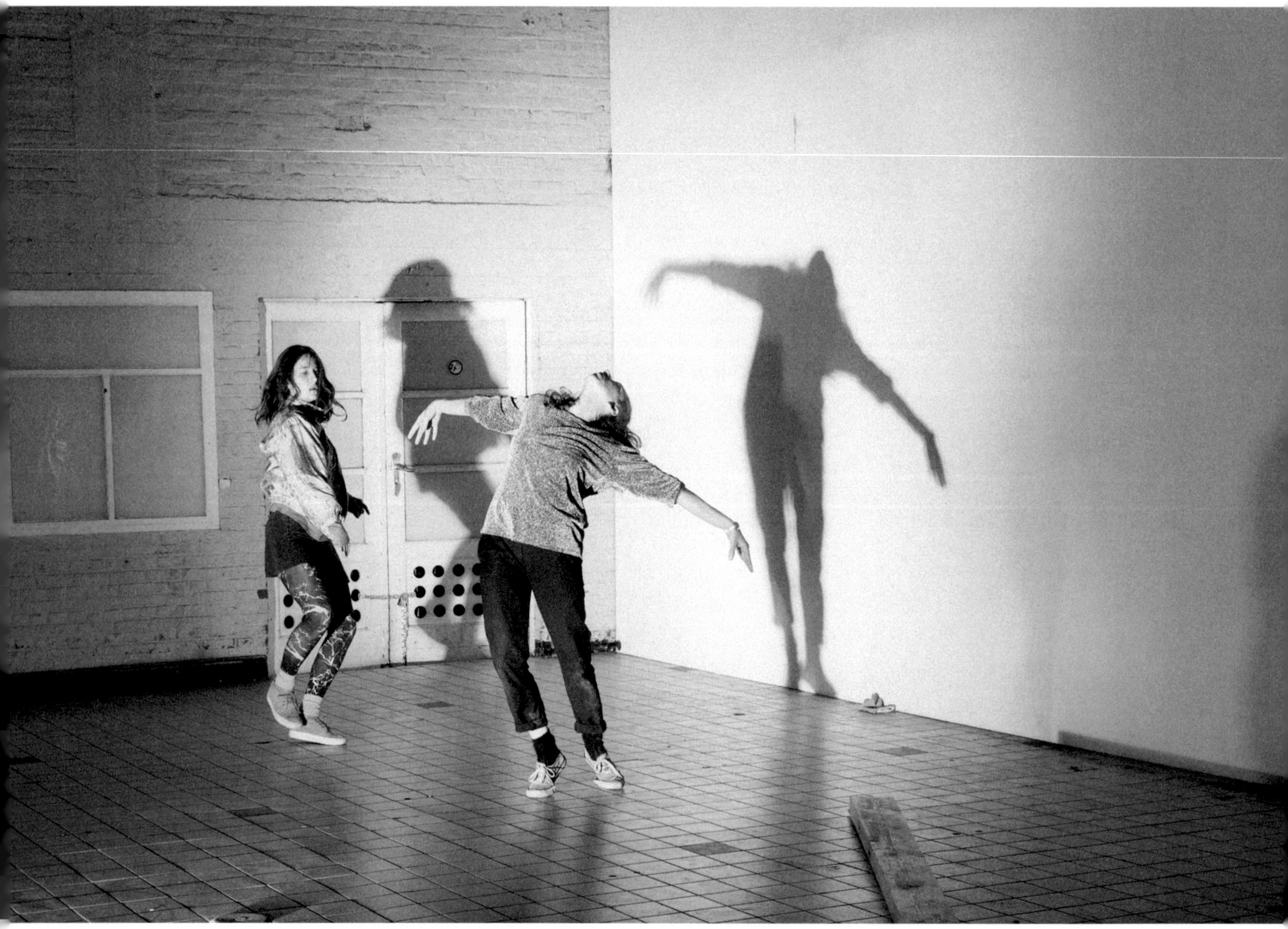

[322] ▀ MARA
Monica Mays

↓P154

[227] ▄ Instant Composition
Common Contribution

↓P148

[091] 20H48 Workshop: Improvised Spaces
Gauthier Chambry
↓P138

[444] Port Nord
Common Contribution
↓P160

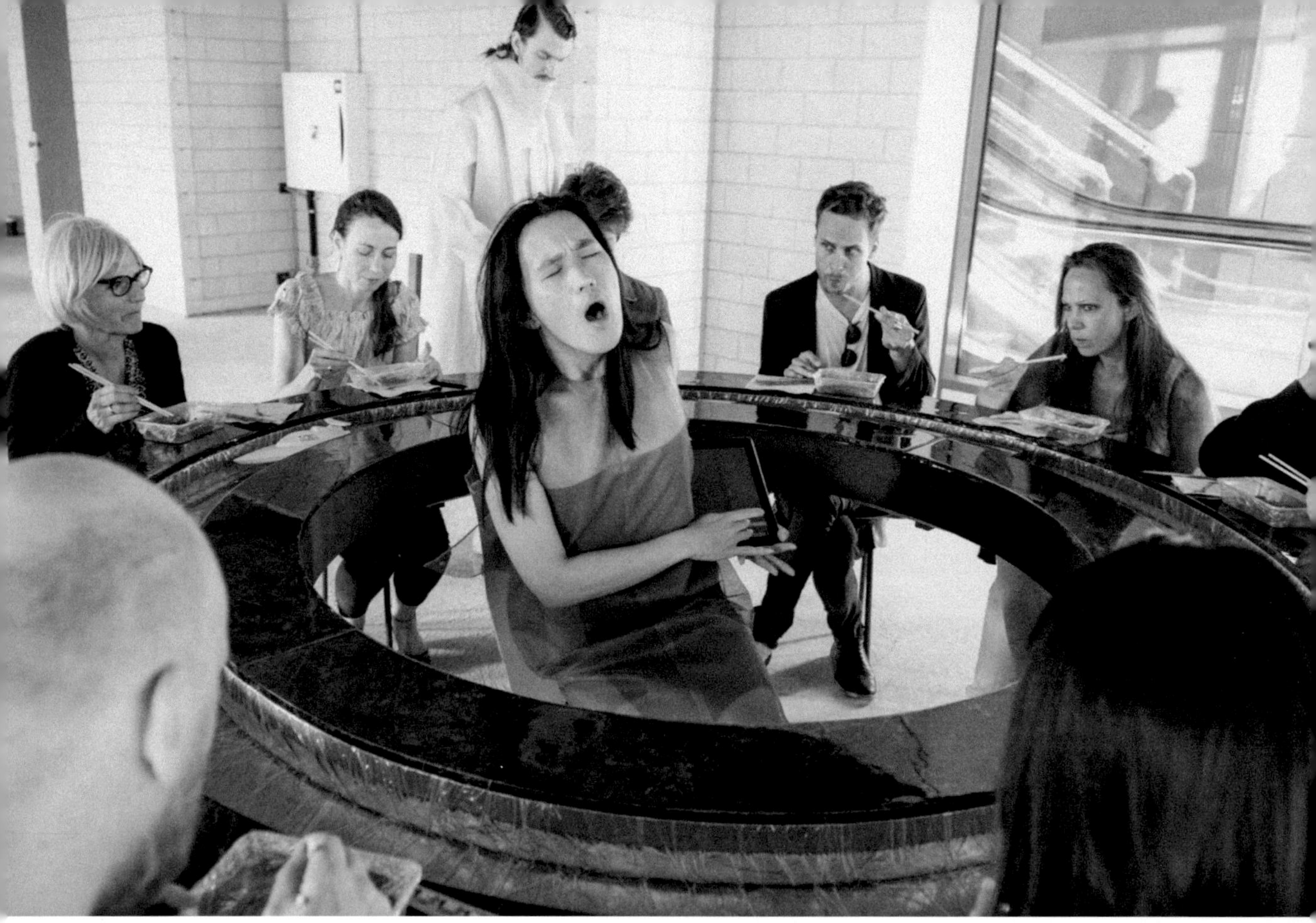

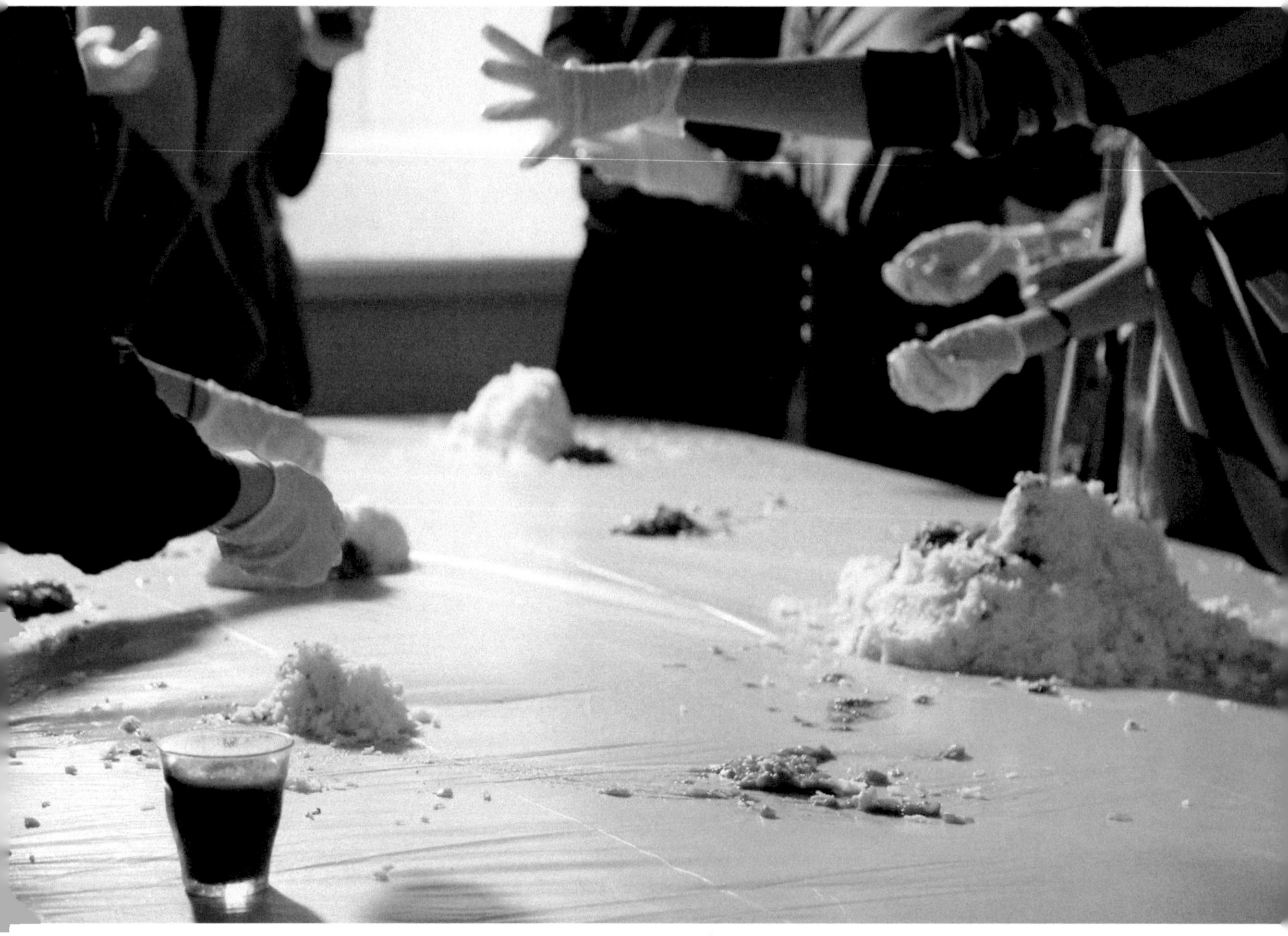

[312] ▀ Hero's Banquet
Shih-Hui Hung

↓P152

[234] ▄ Instant Composition
Common Contribution

↓P148

[204] ■ Commoning the Bread
Antoine Guay
↓P146

[279] ■ Nagele by Nagele
Common Contribution
↓P150

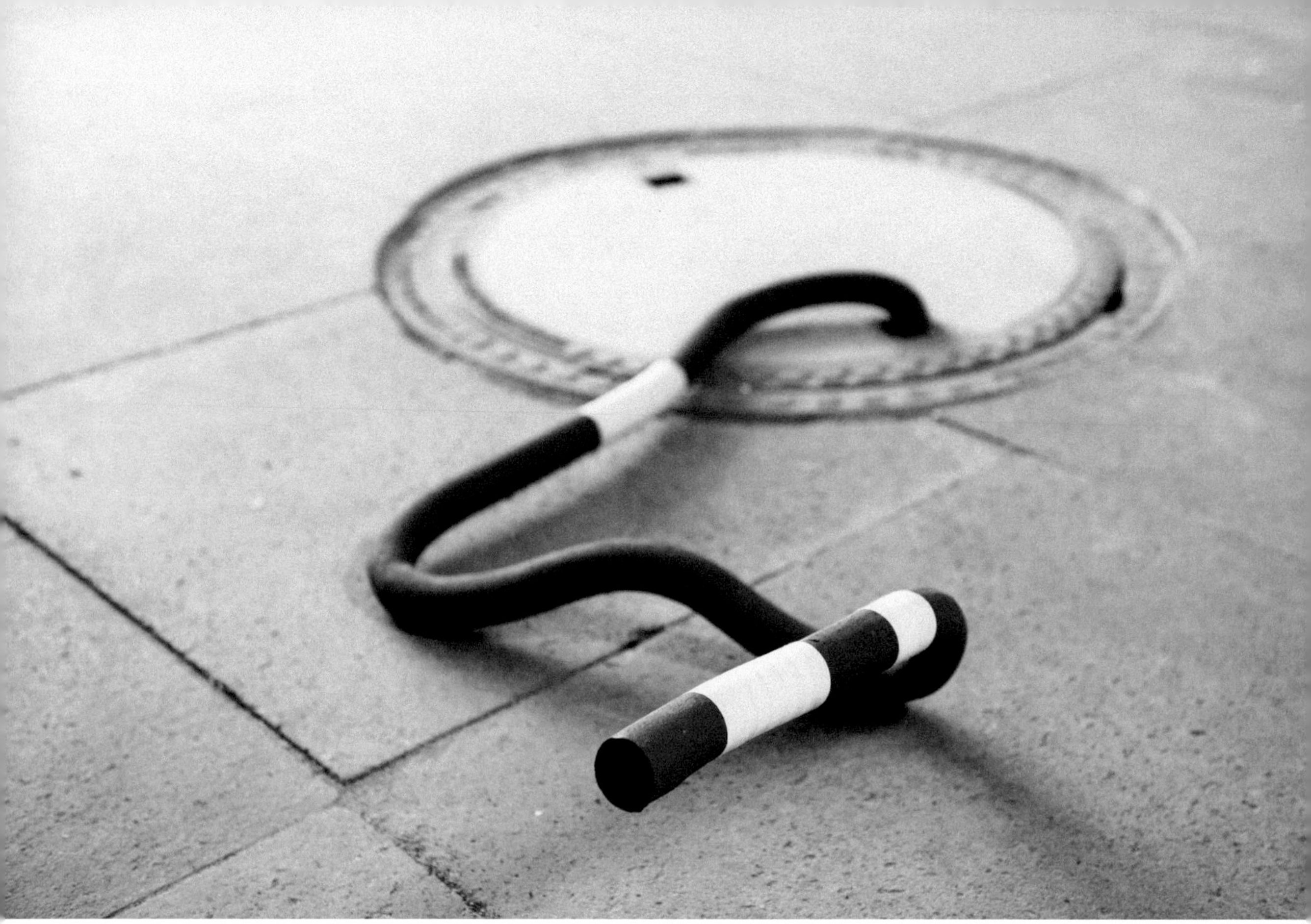

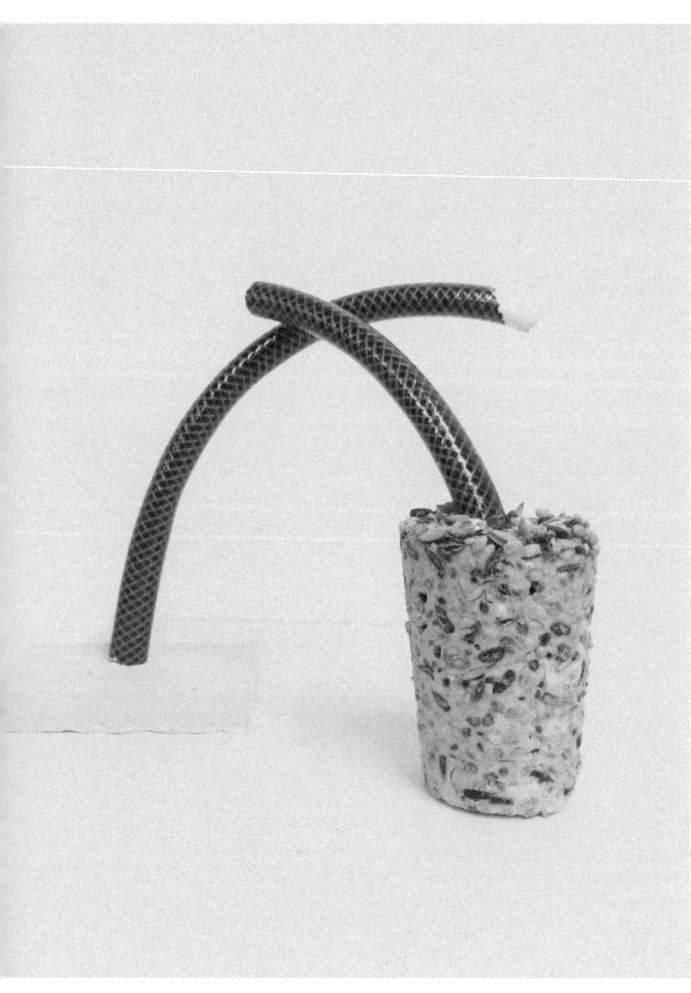

[304] ■ Else Here (Process as Station)
Carolin Gießner

[indv] ■ Beeing with Birds
Malissa Anne Canez Sabus

 ↓P152

[209] ■ Chei Del Fouq
Francesca Lucchitta
↓P146

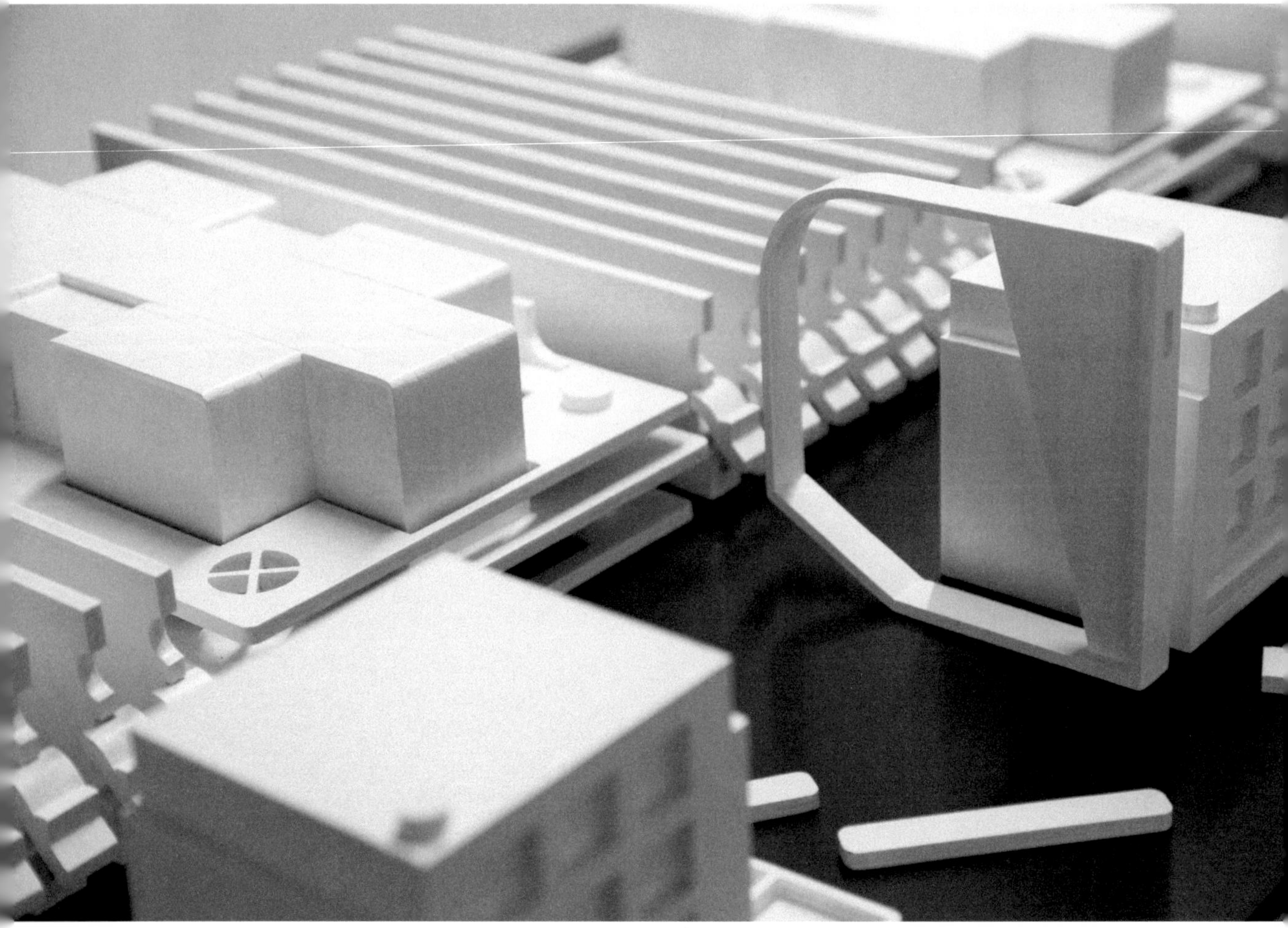

[305] ■ Making a Living
Eva Hoonhut
↓P152

[068] ◨ No Name (Case Study)
Ruben Mols
↓P138

[200] ◼ As the cupboard ist to the home,
       so the home is to the cupboard
       Elia Castino

[017] ◼ At Capacity Contribution
       Rein Verhoef

↓P146   ↓P136   101

[113] ■ Unconditional Void
Rein Verhoef

[121] ■ The Fabric of Sound
Common Contribution

↓P142

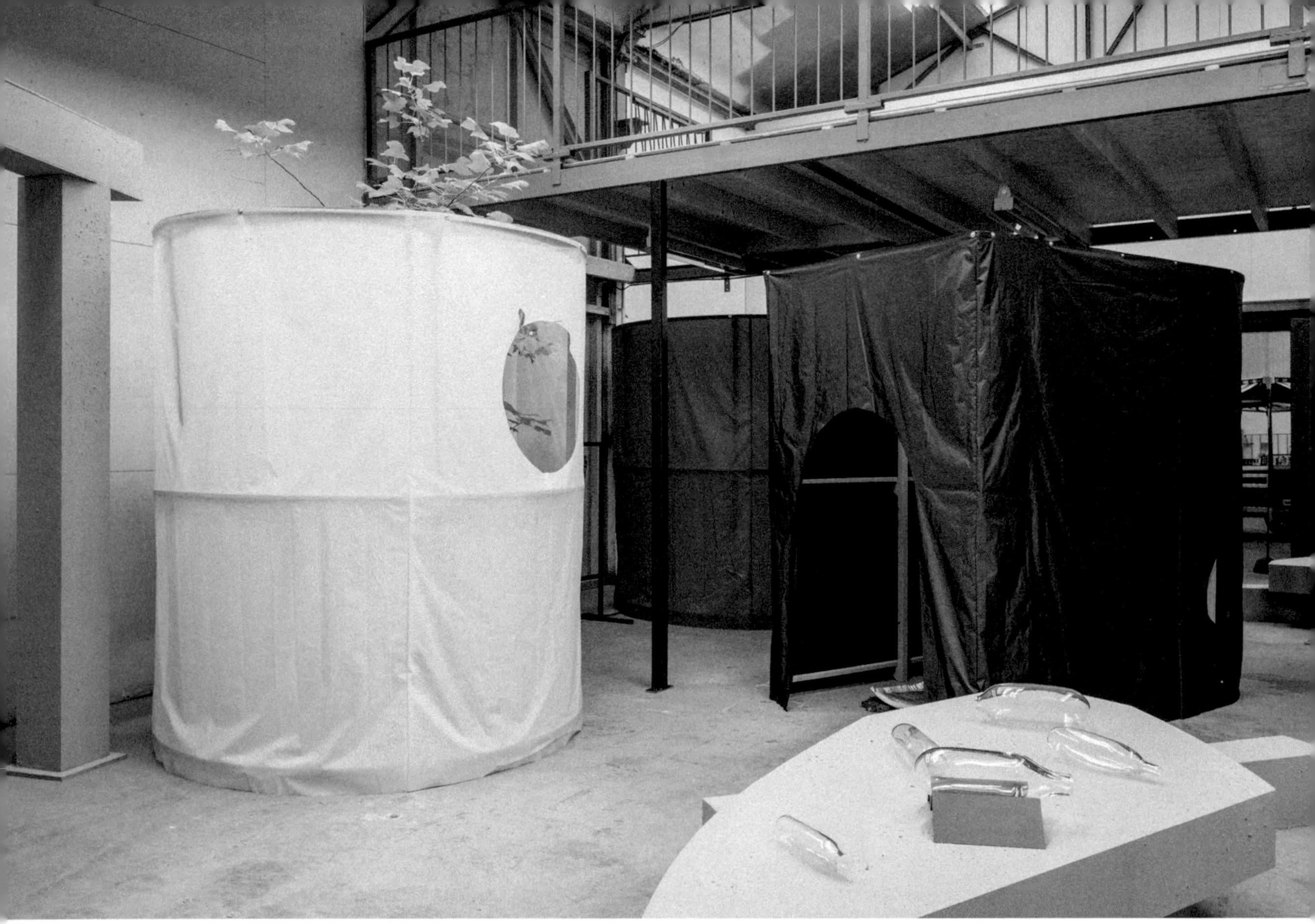

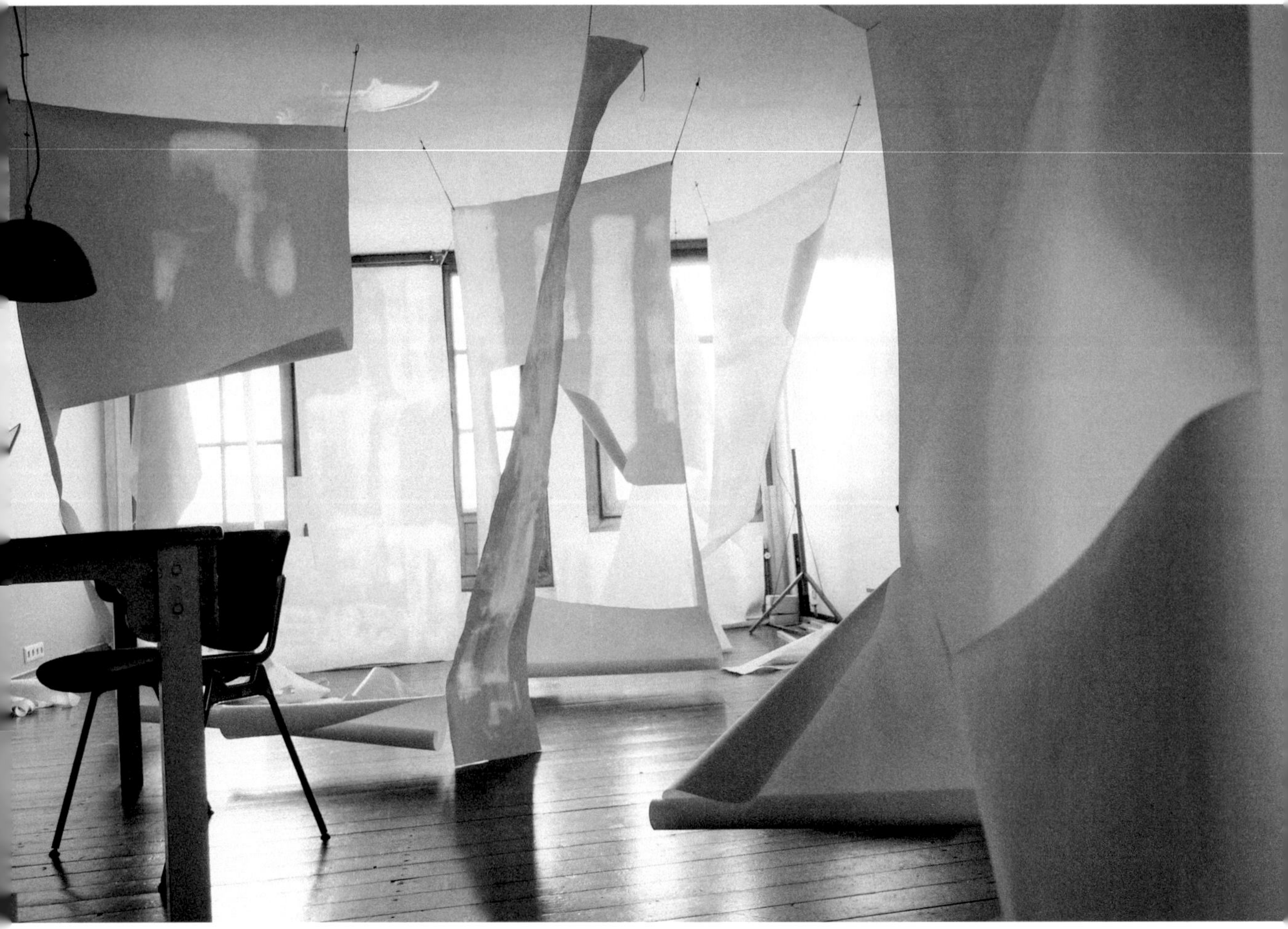

[099] ⬒ Encampment of other Spaces
Samuel Kuhfuss Gustavsen

[indv] ⬓ Towards Melancholic Spaces
Malissa Anne Canez Sabus

↓P140

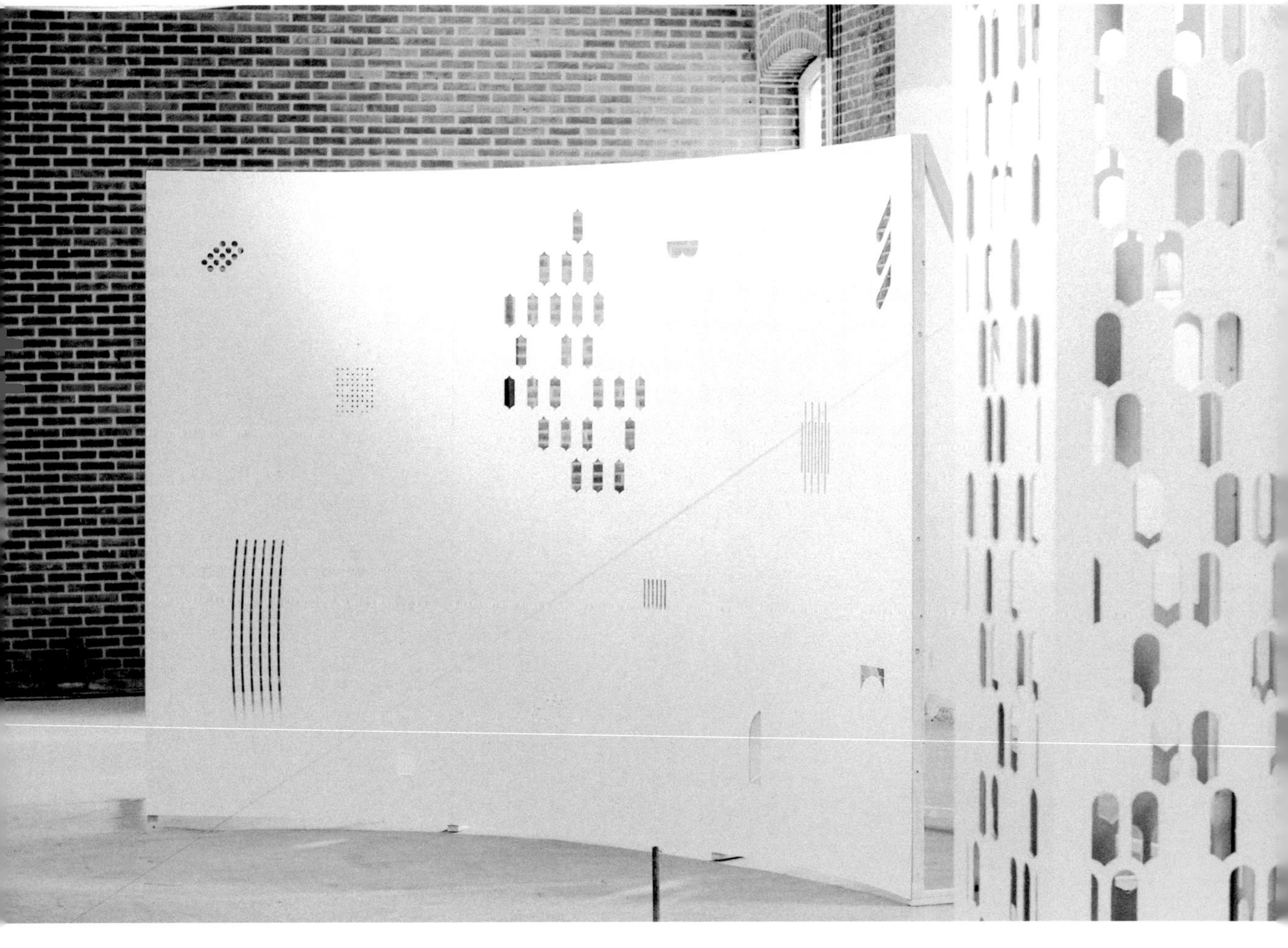

[101] ■ Jelly Coasts and Milk Rivers
Liene Pavloska
↓P140

[486] ■ Salsa Contribution
Samuel Kuhfuss Gustavsen
↓P162

[088] ■ Domestication
Niels Albers

[344] ■ Boy
Kristoffer Zeiner Christiansen
↓P154

[069] ■ Celebration of Liberation (Case Study)
Roman Takchenko
↓P138

107

[316] ■ We stare Series
Lily Lanfermeijer
↓P152

[475] ■ Reclaim after Reclaim
Common Contribution
↓P162

[293] ■ I Am Therefore
        Nadjim Bigou

[592] ■ Unequal Club
        Common Contribution

↓ P152   ↓ P168   109

[212] ■ Capillary Malformation
Davide-Christelle Sanvee

↓P146

[222] ■ Infrastructure of Intimacy Contribution
Gauthier Chambry

↓P148

[094] Descending Downwards
Naomi Credé

↓P140

[275] Monument to my Mother Contribution
Liene Pavlovska

↓P150

111

[294] ■ Drive-In Landscape
Hein van Duppen
↓P152

[433] ■ Pick-Up Contribution
Maria Mazzanti
↓P160

[218] ■ Heterogenous Waters [indv] ■ Be Piet
Elizaveta Strakhova Davide-Christelle Sanvee

↓P146

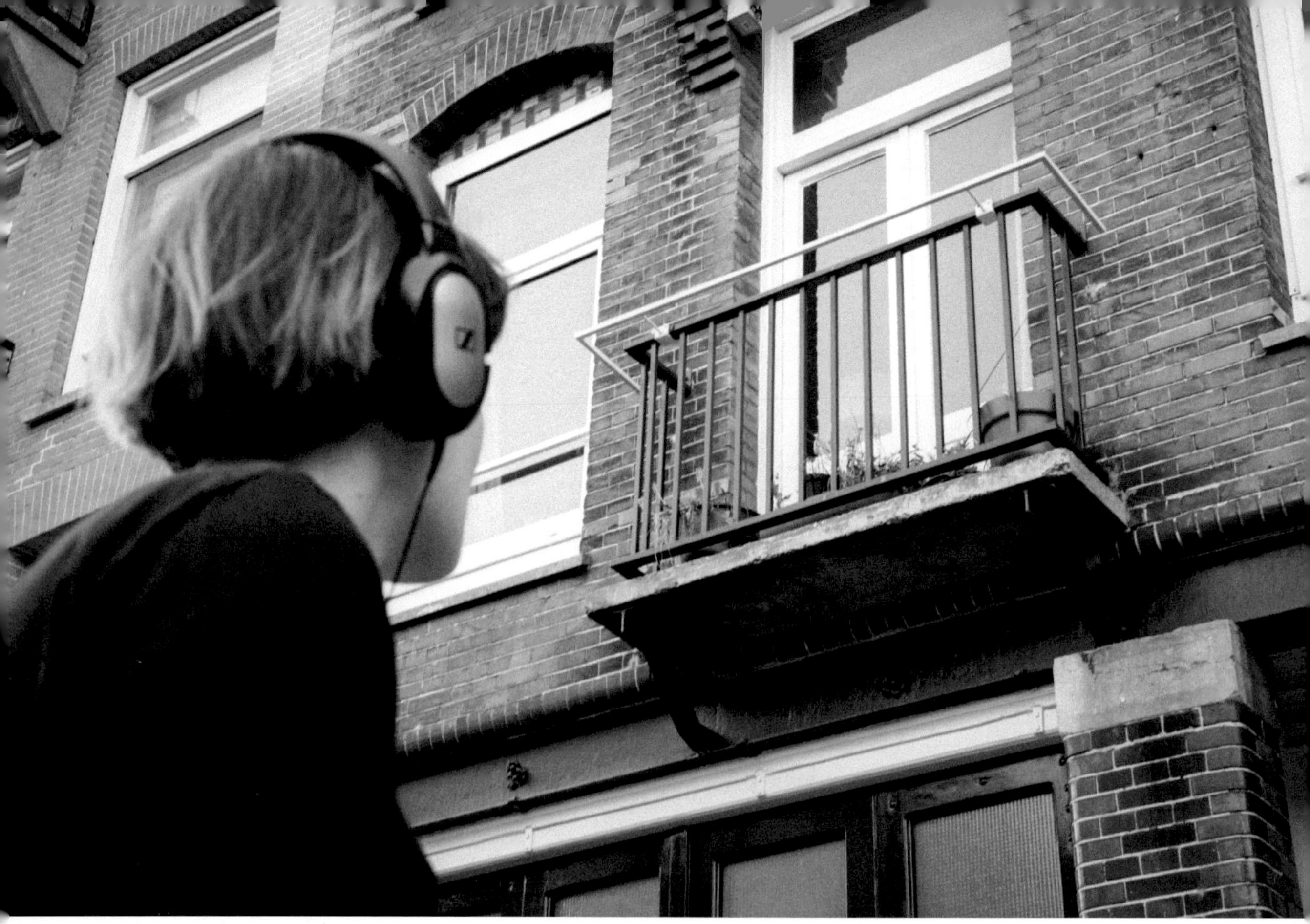

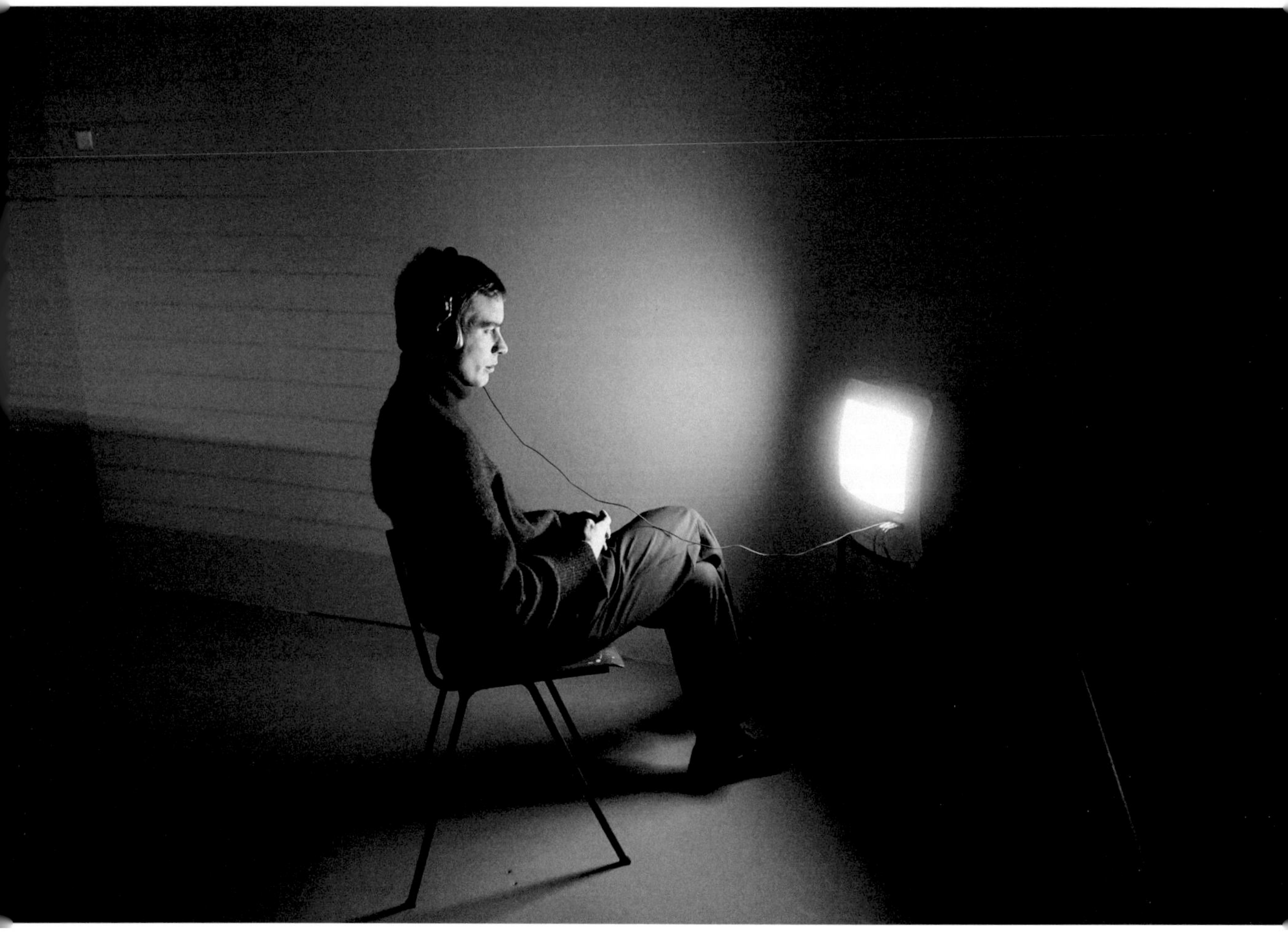

[213] ■ Everything around, including you
Maike Statz

[616] ■ Zoomscape Contribution
Kyulim Kim and Beatriz Conefrey

↓P146

↓P168

[484] ■ Salsa Contribution
Liene Pavlovska
↓P162

[384] ■ The Height of the Balustrade (One to One)
Maike Statz
↓P156

[197] ■ Unreal Estates: The Tale of Liberty Hills [062] ■ Case Study Contribution
Andrea Belosi   Thorben Gröbel
↓P146   ↓P138

[341] ■ Dealing with Control　　　　　　　[619] ■ Zoomscape
　　　　Neeltje ten Westenend　　　　　　　　　　Common Contribution
↓P154　　　　　　　　　　　　　　　　↓P168

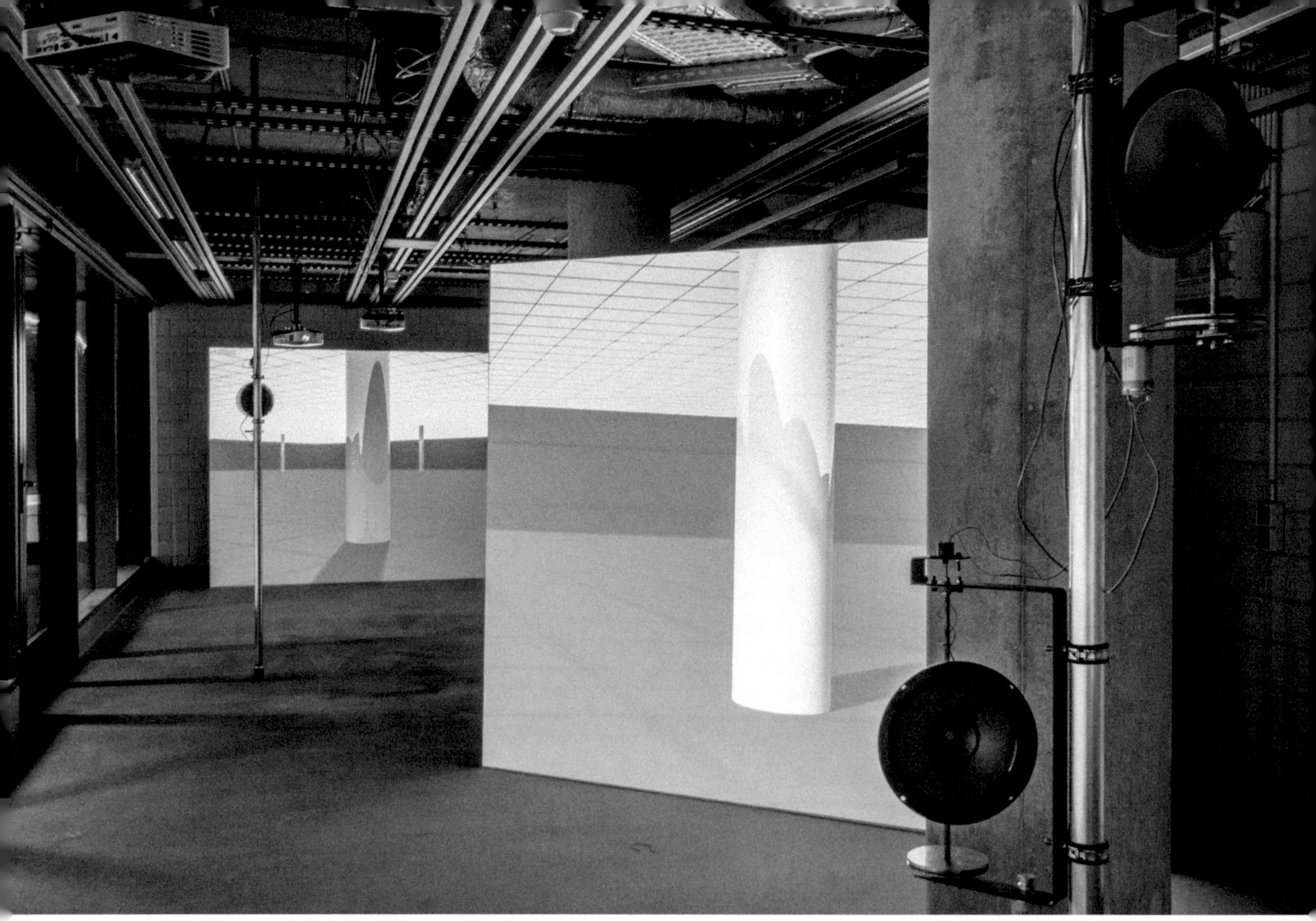

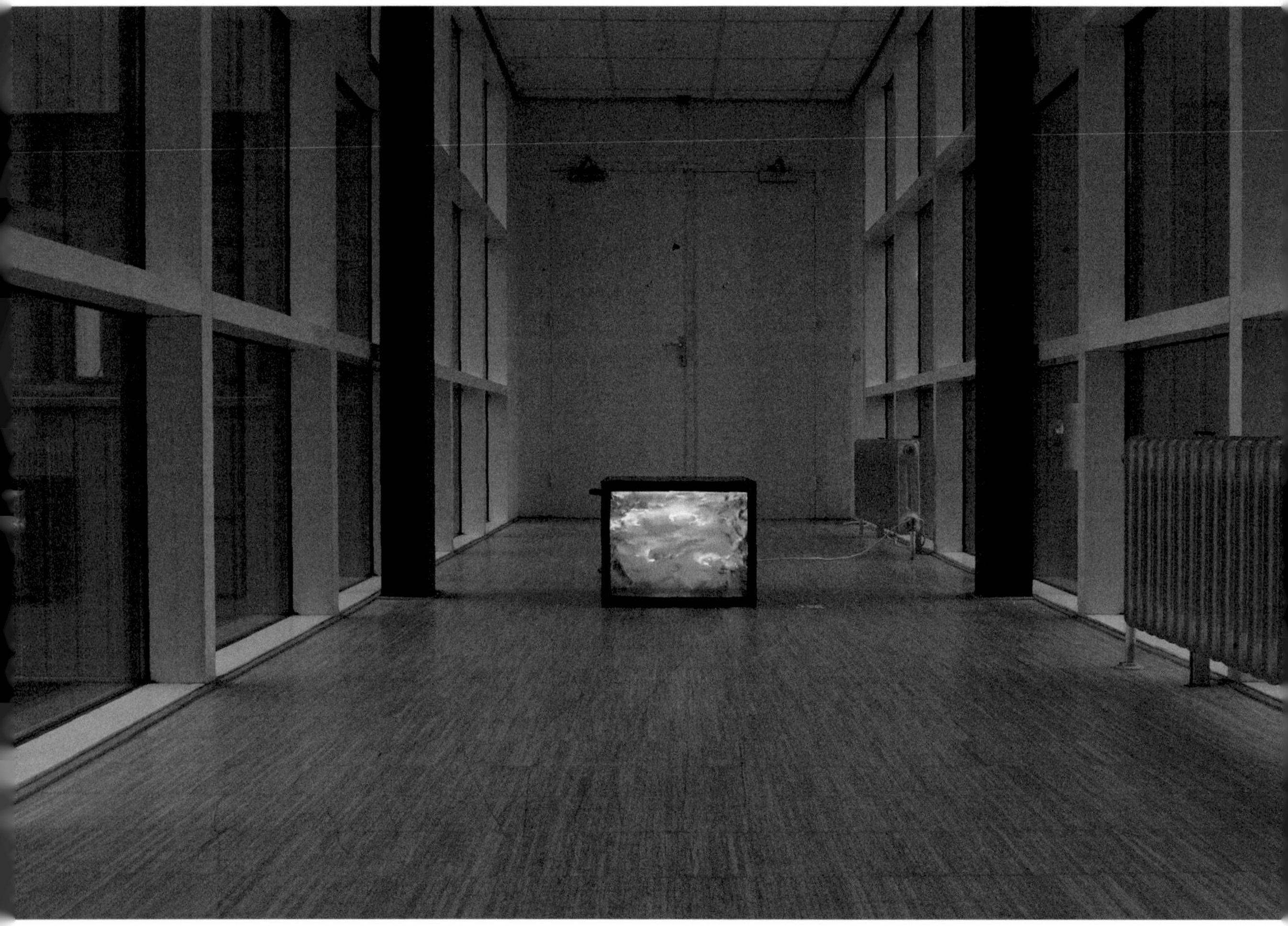

[328] ■ And Notes Of, Blush-Pepper
Aaro Murphy

↓P154

[053] ■ What is beyond the Dikes? (Case Study)
Kyulim Kim

↓P138

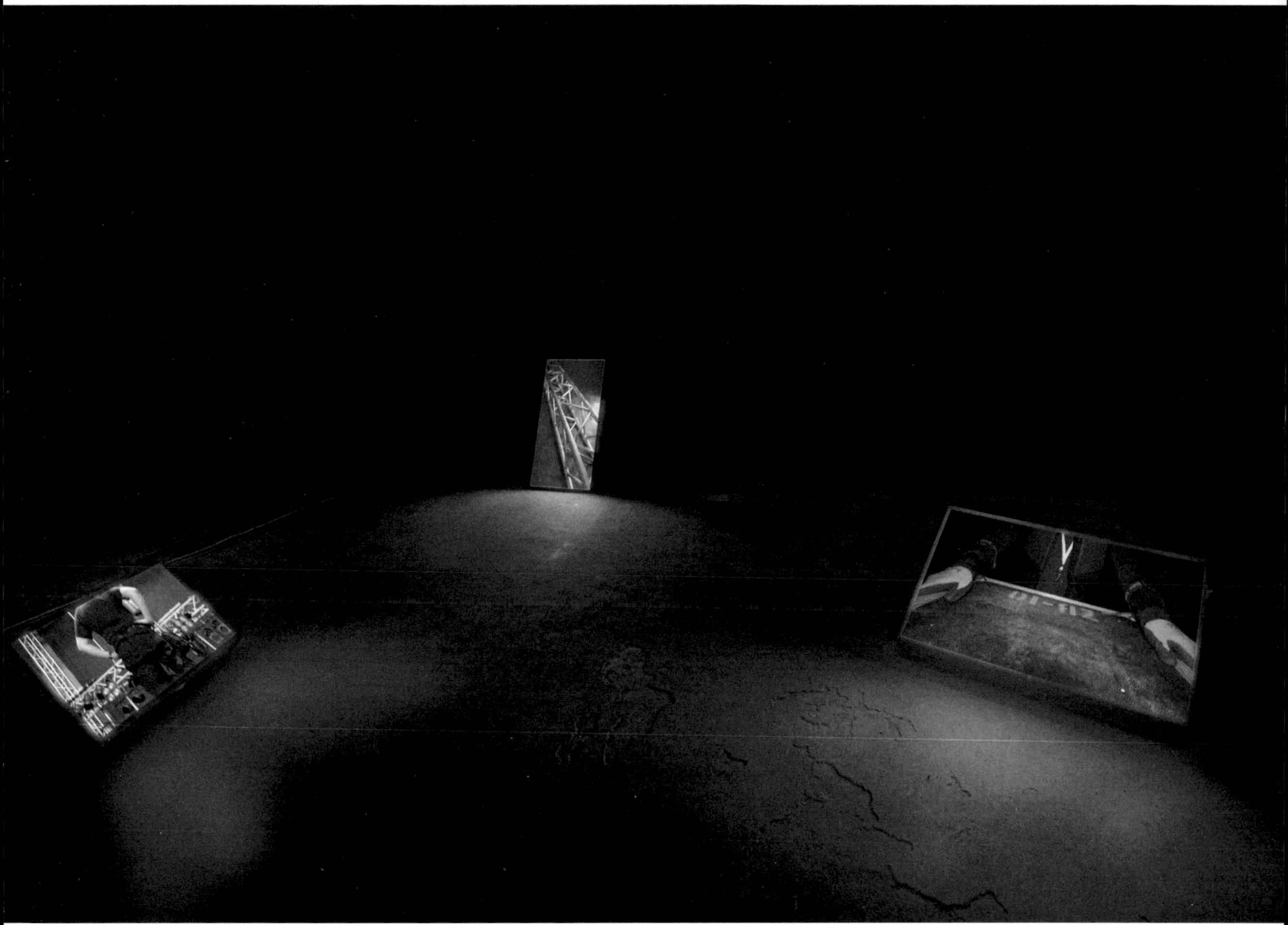

[107] ■ TBD
Mirko Podkowik
↓P140

[332] ■ Prepwork
Mirko Podkowik
↓P154

119

● **Exploring the Frontiers of Spatial Production**

Lukas Feireiss

Rural flatlands, the twilight of suburbia, and gritty city settings. Mediterranean shorelines and Alpine Mountainscapes. Open-pit mines and industrial legacies. Abandoned buildings and unfinished infrastructures. Harbors, airports and refugee camps.

Embracing a truly global approach, these are but a few of the peculiar places of production of the Studio for Immediate Spaces directed by Swiss architect Leopold Banchini at the Sandberg Instituut, Amsterdam between 2016 and 2019. Constantly crossing and deliberately ignoring borders, this nomadic studio has always been in passage from one place to the next. Thereby all of these places share a common setting, which is nothing less than the world.

The book at hand now offers a glimpse into this unique journey around the globe. Equally assuming the role of geographer, researcher, architect, urban planner and designer, we here witness the studio's participants explore the very frontiers of spatial production today. All of their works are testimony to an intensive examination and shaping of the environments that they inhabit and in which they co-exist. They are also poetic interventions that interfere with given situations and thereby challenge preconceived notions of space by providing alternative viewpoints that allow for deliberate shifts in perspective. Interventions in both the built as well as the natural environment that range from small to large scale, ephemeral to permanent, playful to formal, and from individual to collective actions. By elevating often neglected spatial contexts and constraints, the Studio for Immediate Spaces thereby draws attention to the rapidly changing ways of life in today's global realities.

Despite the great diversity of approaches, all of the projects are in one way or the other also conjoined in their affirmative endeavor to transform abstract spaces to concrete places. This deliberate alternation and oscillation of the former to the latter can be described very simply as the process in which a particular part of our spatial environment is being activated, inhabited and cohabited with an added value of experience and meaning. A modus operandi or exercise, that allows for both an individual and intimate as well as a collective and shared appropriation of our environment and life on an aesthetic, functional, social and political level.

> Rather than to describe space from a mono-functional perspective as a geographically localized and static area, space is here understood as an ever-changing altered state within the fabric of our lives — where multiple realities of constant change play a critical and vital role in the natural formation and transformation of our environment. Beyond urbanism and architectural conventions, the Studio for Immediate Spaces considers space via its discursive and insight-generating qualities as an alternative site of creation and cultural production. It advocates the generation and facilitation of immediate spaces that act as flexible frameworks for multiple opportunities and possibilities of social, political and cultural nature.

The Studio

 **Get Lost**

Leopold Banchini
Director of the Studio for Immediate Spaces
from 2016 to 2019

"Who Are You and What Are You Thinking?" was the curious name of Harold Cohen's first exercise with his students at Carbondal (Southern Illinois University of Carbondale, 1955–1970). Aiming to shake the very notion of design, the students were dropped in the wilderness for 72 hours with 10 bucks and an emergency whistle. Are there such things as universal needs and can education radically question preconceived notions of what architecture needs to be? To figure this out, one must escape the safe environment of the academical world undeniably homogenous and privileged. Identity politics seems to monopolize today's art schools' internal debates and conflicts, often failing to emancipate outside of its boundaries. In order to regain agency towards a world where class struggles are raging and economics only seem to decide the future of our environment, it is urgent to escape the white cube.

For three years we travelled across territories and got lost. With a fresh eye, we tried to get a sense of the landscapes created by our contemporary neo-liberal society. These landscapes that exist just behind the walls of the touristic city centers, yet are so rarely depicted. We believed in affinity groups and their strengths, no matter how different the backgrounds. We tried to build trust and followed personal intuitions and artistic expression. Without predefined methods and on the outskirts of the traditional disciplines, we questioned the possibility of a new path, neither architecture nor art, neither commercial nor philanthropic, radically aware of the ecological and social disaster about to burst from the shiny crust of our privilege surroundings. Now we can admit that we didn't find a single easy path but that we opened many difficult ones. No answers or methods, rather questions and experiences. But what is education without getting lost?

Starting these 3 years we tried to redefine the existence of the Studio with a set of intentions. We defined them as follows: One, the Studio will investigate the spaces too often neglected by the traditional architecture and interior architecture education. Two, the Studio will focus on the spaces created by our contemporary culture without the help of professionals (informal, temporary, social, virtual, immediate). Three, the Studio will be equally interested in the social conditions and the political context of spaces as in their architectonic components. Four, the Studio will analyse these spaces through artistic research and with the help of DIY and hands-on production methods of investigation. Five, the Studio will learn from the genius of neo-vernacular and the beauty of collective intelligence and popular cultures. Six, the Studio will promote an interdisciplinary approach but will value the specific tools developed by spatial disciplines. Seven, the Studio will constantly produce full-scale immediate spaces through experiments, workshops, common and individual projects.

Now reaching the end of our three year mandate, we can wonder if we managed to stick to our educational program. More importantly, we can be critical towards it and start all over again. This is the aim of this publication. It is hard to tell the tale of this trip through a short selection of images, but the students of the Hochschule für Grafik und Buchkunst in Leipzig, with their fresh eye, are giving us their version. Through attempts of classification, they defined five reoccurring steps in our exercises, the backbone of an intention, almost a method. They defined them as follow:

● *STATUS-QUO*
●● *IN-SITU*
●●● *TALK-OVER*
●●●● *BUILD-UP*
●●●●● *AFTERMATH*

A love from outer space: some thoughts about neo-vernacular spaces and the importance of reclaiming space

Marie-Avril Berthet
Tutor in the Studio for Immediate Spaces
from 2016 to 2019

I have long been a loyal fan to A Love from Outer Space, the dj duet composed of Andrew Weatherhall and Sean Johnston. I love pretty much every bit of the music these two monuments of British rave culture play individually. But when they dj together there is really something special happening. As in something spatial and something cosmic. The way they stage and embody this idea of a force coming from space that would have the power to trickle down and infuse a crowd of dancers into collective love really is powerful. And I can tell you, you know which space you inhabit when the spell is in action. On numerous occasions, they got me to think about an interesting contradiction I see, between the mainstream idea of space on the one hand, and the reality of space on the other. "Space", often enough, is thought of as something that is "out there", above us, something mysterious and somehow magical, something that we look at with fascination. But something we have no agency over. When, if you think of our human reality, space is the one dimension of everyday life that is the most tangible and the most designed. And most importantly, someone does designs the spaces we live in. For a purpose. "Everyday life space" is far from mysterious. It is the most down to earth aspect of our lives.

    Feminist Geographer Doreen Massey, who has inspired so much of the interesting critical geography in the last three decades, was a "space advocate". In her views, the dichotomy between "space" and "place", for example, is highly problematic. Space, in the common language, is the bare physical environment that we live in, she says. When you say of a flat, "Oh, it's a nice space", the flat in question is somehow defined by the void, the emptiness that there is between the walls surrounding it, rather than by thinking, well, who placed these walls? Who circumscribed this space? And for what reason? Unlike space, "place" is the sentiment and attachment we associate with certain spaces, the history, the meaning-making, that moment when a house becomes a home. This dichotomy is fundamentally political, Massey says, because it strips space down to something that we have no agency over. It is as if bathrooms were "naturally" designed by interior designers and houses by architects; as if only engineers had the power to reshape mountains; as if it was the logical course of history for empires to come out of the ground so that they could be studied by geographers. And what about non-space-specialists? There is a whole literature on urban social movements. But how can we even aspire to cities to be socially just places to live if we cannot even think that we are part of the process of designing them?

Before I started teaching in the SIS, I had a long conversation with Leopold to try and circumscribe what exactly the course would focus on and what kind of contribution the geographer that I am could bring into the course. Leopold and I have long shared interests: we look at, think about and try our best to design spaces, which have potential to disrupt the mainstream conception of space, spaces which are subversive, spaces which are irreverent to spatial order, spaces of hedonism and, probably the most important of all, spaces that people build themselves, for fun, because it better serves them than by necessity. Following the thread of our interest in self-built spaces, the term vernacular inevitably came up in the conversation.

I myself research subcultures and counter-cultures and specifically their contributions to the making of cities. In this regard, I am used to talking about alternative spaces or DIY spaces. But vernacular spaces are not subcultural spaces. A subculture involves a group of people who associate themselves with a certain set of cultural aesthetics and cultural practices. They often dress the same way, share their musical taste, etc. Vernacular doesn't necessitate collective action. A unique piece of pottery or a garment can be vernacular. So to this extent, I guess, vernacular almost means "crafted" or "artisanal". The idea of a vernacular space, indeed, has in common with the representation of a subcultural space to be made by those and for those who inhabit it. Another important difference is that "subcultural" somehow refers to now and the contemporary cultural world, whereas "vernacular" is tinted with the idea of a pre-industrial way of making things. We weren't interested in tradition, so neo-vernacular made more sense for us.

The one dimension of vernacularism that stuck with us is that it is most often used in relation to architecture to describe constructions designed by non-architects. If you type in "vernacular architecture" in a search engine, you mostly get images of constructions such as huts, shacks and cabins or, generally speaking, traditional buildings: stone and clay houses, half-timbering structures, thatched roofs, etc. Most vernacular architecture is light, low-tech and is achievable by hand. Generally speaking, vernacular constructions are considered like a "heritage". In the Western world though, it will be like a taster of the past, unlike in the global South, where, the chances are, it will be glorified like a perpetuated art. Vernacular, to this extent, implies a hierarchy in space design: it situates non-specialist architecture in relation to architect-made architecture. It also reveals design hierarchies between the Western world and the global South. Geographically or socially, vernacular implies spaces designed by people are not part of the "cultural elites". That is very powerful.

Lately, vernacular has timidly made a reappearance as an alternative qualification for precarious and informal housing: understand slums. This phenomenon is interesting and disturbing. The use of the term vernacular in this context indeed betrays both the desire and the discomfort to express positive views over urban forms, which sadly emerge from profound social injustice, but nonetheless are fascinating for their complete amateurism. There is obviously a real risk to glorify "neo-vernacular" architectures without considering the tragic social context from which they emerge. It is equally important to recognise that entirely self-built environments are captivating because, in a way, they remind us that cities are nothing more than something we can build even without permission, even without cranes and most importantly even without capital.

And so, how did the idea of neo-vernacular spaces guide my way in the Studio for Immediate Spaces? First, I have to say, vernacular helped me connect space with the idea of immediacy. The temporality of geography, too often, is almost beyond the human life span. And having neo-vernacular spaces as a work frame triggered a lot of thoughts around the temporality of space and the power of reclaiming spaces, which are designed within a short timeframe. The more I think of it, the more I find the narrative around old stones and "monuments" to carry along a profoundly conservative vision of cities. Immediately built spaces are not inherently socially just, don't get me wrong. If you think of Dubai or Hong Kong, you don't exactly get a picture of a city that people have more agency over. But vernacular spaces can't be made for profit like skyscrapers are because they respond to people's needs here and now. They are not fancy commodities since they are designed by and for those who use them. Self-design is still a core aspect of how neo-vernacular could have the potential to generate more empowering spaces, in my views. There is something about how a self-built space completely eludes the commodification of space, but at the same time is a positive affirmation of the existence of its designer(s). For me, the dancefloor continues to be the epitome of a neo-vernacular space. It is a social space as much as a designed space. Or maybe it is the point where they merge. It is forever reproduced but also always different because it doesn't exist without the momentum that brings people together by the power of the out-of-space love. The sound system is an architecture but most of it is invisible. You get an embodied experience of it but only if others are alongside you. In a way, the dancefloor is a space of total collective agency.

As I am trying to conclude on these thoughts, a friend posts the set of Bambii, a young DJ who is reviewed as follows: "Bambii is one of Canada's most compelling DJs. Whether online or on dancefloors, her political and musical vernacular give credence to dance music's ever expanding reach, and the relationships it helps forge between individuals, cultures and spaces." We're clearly just at the beginning of rethinking how space and political agency connect. But if vernacular is embodied by a young Canadian born black woman who embarks hundreds of dancers in a swirl of collective fun, I am on board with that.

The Studio

● **(Re)Framing Space**
　　Vision for the future of the studio

Julian Schubert and Ludwig Engel
Co-directors of the Studio for
Immediate Spaces from September 2019

Everything manifests in space. Migration is about space, ecology is about space, equality is about space. Space is political, economic, social and aesthetic. At the Studio for Immediate Spaces at the Sandberg Instituut we deal with space, how it is produced, how it is used, occupied, and freed. Though, what exactly is space? For us, space is both a theoretical entity and a real thing that inform one another. To deal with space means to deal in space. To deal in space one needs to understand space as a form of discourse as well as the realm of action in the real world.

To bridge theory and practice one needs knowledge, tools and courage: Knowledge, to know what is possible. Tools, to know how to actually do it. Courage, to push through towards execution. To achieve this, the Studio for Immediate Spaces fosters collaboration in the studio as it is practiced in reality. It prefers the collective effort of making space to an alleged genius gesture of the individual master, developing an alternative spatial practice—independent, collaborative, relevant. The studio is meant for those, who want to practice what is neither the private architect as servant of capital nor the free artist depending on the goodwill of capital.

Facing a collapse of ecological systems, a widening gap between rich and poor, between avant-garde and the mass, between insiders and outsiders, the Studio for Immediate Spaces aims at exploring, investigating and shaping a spatial practice different from how it is commonly taught in architecture and urban planning schools, focused on the genesis and production of contemporary spatial configurations. Since its founding, the studio has invited (and will continue to do so) 'undisciplinary spatialists', who's ambition is to design, plan, test, and eventually adapt and build spaces, confronting ecological urgencies and social inequalities with new spatial concepts.

The political ambition of the studio is to be(come) a spatially relevant agent. The primary purpose of the Sandberg Instituut is to nurture autonomy and freedom in the students' individual practices, enabling them to develop as artists in a world of general uncertainty. To this extent the Studio for Immediate Spaces holds a special position between being a spatial agent critiquing and questioning (possibly even changing) the context it works in by engaging with non-academic and non-artistic actors in the urban realm and developing a practice that is informed by an artist's uncompromised and autonomous perspective reconnecting agent and agency in a time when spatial experts that look at the world proactively and productively are so direly needed.

We believe that change for the better is always possible. That the city as the ultimate space to live together is not the problem, but the solution to a common, socially, ecologically and economically sound society. But to transform what more than often now feels like a contested space into a space for exchange, communication and humanity, it needs an open eye to see what is happening, an ear to the ground to understand what is being said, curiosity to venture into unknown and foreign territory and expand one's own view of the world. We imagine the Studio for Immediate Spaces to be a laboratory for spatial practice that does open up to urban actors and tests spatial ideas that have relevance for how we live today and how we want to live tomorrow.

● **Real Architects**

Fabulous Future
Artist collective created
in 2018 by students of
the Studio for Immediate Spaces

Now — Seven faces illuminated by the faint light of their computers as the sun sets in the distance, a small house surrounded by darkening pink skies and a dull Dutch landscape. We're sat on sofas surrounding a table laid with tepid tea and the remains of chocolate, in a holiday home, made for seven. We've removed ourselves for the weekend from our studio in one of the most expensive parts of the Netherlands and travelled thirty-four minutes north of Amsterdam to spend time together. Fake architects in a fake traditional Dutch house. Everything here is for seven: seven spots on the sofa (two on the short side, three on the long side, plus the two armchairs), seven beds, of course, seven chairs around the dining table and seven chairs on the terrace. A simulation of a small town, as real as unreal. We're here to think about work, friendship, future goals. To talk about the big picture and the bigger thoughts. Telepathy is high today.

> *Then* — I had quickly googled some of the people whose names I could figure out from their email addresses, but everything seems so different now. Are we competing, are we partners in crime? Is this genuine or is this a strategy? We gather and get close to each other. Really close. A bit closer, different nationalities, different ages, different stories and different experiences. A bit closer until we are a uniform blob of people.
>
> What time is it now? Who is next on the list? Oh, we're running late. Did you hear from them? Where are they? They just sent a message to say that they're late. Oh, then we can swap with them. We can also move them to tomorrow.
>
> Most of the group sits down or leans against something now. Everybody is quiet and listens. Ideas traveled from one to the other, we took care of each other, things worked, things didn't work. Points of view entangled that even the most painstaking combing couldn't unravel. Not now though. But what does it mean to be critical? Does it wish to help or hurt? Is it meant to enlighten or does it somehow seek revenge?
>
> We start jumping on the spot. Up and down and up and down. Jump, jump, jump. There is constant body contact with at least one or two other people, maybe even five. Jumping and slowly moving through each other.

Ah, oh, there you are, it's you. You're next. Ok? Where should we sit? I'll be there in one minute. I'll be there in a bit. Ok. How are you? Should we sit here? Or should we sit here at the big table? Would you rather sit over there?

    I'm on a train again, it's a train I've never been on before. Two rows of windows on each side framing the swiss alps in the distance. This one was a strange one. I was the first one to go. I packed my stuff in my backpack and prepared all the snow gear for my hike down the night before. In the morning I slipped out of the snoring room, got my stuff and started walking down. Later you're rushing down the mountain, attempting to run downwards through the snow, slipping and sliding, losing a sense of the ground beneath our feet. What could appear in the morning mist?

    I used to arrive at 7:30 am, curated table, shifting positions and over-caffeinated shaky hands for cutting the perfect edge. You spent all day building yourself a den to concentrate, but I've yet to see you sit inside and work, instead, you lie there — motionless, shouting something in a language I can't understand.

    Institutional disposition towards quantitative didactic value. Frustrated, we began to dance instead. Hummus gatherings, bending backwards on the broken chair, stale air; a mixing of pop and grunge. There's a feverish energy, not enjoyable and yet not unpleasant. Stale smells, scrunched up sweet packets, mouldy coffee cups and empty beer cans. Exhaustion, anticipation. Feeling like sharing too much — constantly. You read sitting on a soft baggy chair, you read planking on the carpet, I read in-between two palettes.

    You enter through a curtain and walk on top of the table I sit at; steps following the tempo of loud pop music. The first course of tonight's dinner in your hands.

    We are hiding from the cold upstairs in the cinema room. A collage of foldable beds, air mattresses, backpacks and bodies. Sleeping on the floor, sleeping on tables, sleeping in the corner, sleeping behind the screen, sleeping on chairs.

    Sleepy eyes slowly wake up in view of the other. A kitten passes in-between and through the legs, a horse will join for breakfast. We start the mornings by moving, stretching and testing the spaces of our limbs as we move in and around the building, slowly shedding layers as our bodies begin to defrost.

    Movement, construction, eating, drinking. After cleaning up we gather outside the building. You smoke a cigarette, some drink another coffee, some talk, some just enjoy the sunbeams on their skin. Two dancers turns to three, sometimes four. Numerous bodies contained in the factory walls, very occasionally venturing out to buy food, to shower.

    Laying on the sofa, a sickly pale green sheet half hanging off and crumbs lodged in between the cushions. The absurdity of the week prior not yet dawning on us. A moment of care and togetherness is present amidst the chaos.

    Finally out of the hammock tied to the metal beams on the ceiling. Hiding in the silent room, my cave. I've been occupying a table for weeks now. I go and get some bread. Butter and jam are in the fridge that is hung outside the window. A plastic crate fixed to the outside facade, a plank of wood as a lid, it worked quite well in the wintertime. Secret fridge. Secret bed. Secret smoking window.

    It's late in the evening, pitch black outside and unbearably bright neon lights inside. Sitting next to deep water I was alone. Jumping for pleasure, jumping into the unknown. Climbing a ladder to the top following the shadowy silhouette into the glowing light of morning.

This text was produced for this publication collectively by Fabulous Future at a holiday park in Volendam NL, September 2019, reflecting on our time in Studio for Immediate Spaces.

The Studio

● **The House: Moving In**
Maike Statz
Student of the Studio for Immediate Spaces
from 2017 to 2019

The House — I found myself in many places I never expected to be. First Amsterdam. Next the dizzying array of places we travelled to with the department. A group of around 16 people, from varying backgrounds, we would arrive to a specific location and begin the process of orientating or in some cases further disorientating ourselves in order to engage with the project at hand. Arriving became a consistent state of being.

The House was a self-initiated project by the 2017/18 first year participants of Studio for Immediate Spaces. We spent five days inhabiting a vacant house located in the outskirts of Amsterdam within the territory of Schiphol Airport. Responding to the house, the context and the immediate needs of living we established spatial programs, negotiating how to work and live together discreetly. There were multiple moments of arrival to the house. The initial chance discovery of the house by my classmate. Preliminary site visits made at different times by different members of our year group. Finally a more permanent arrival as we began the process of moving in with the intention of staying.

Moving In — Three separate structures occupy the narrow rectangular plot. The 1217m² site was purchased in 2014 by Schiphol Airport as part of a future plan to expand the international airport. Roads pass both in front of and behind the site, which sits between a construction company and a small piece of forested land. On the opposite side of the street is a military base and the state police. The surrounding area hosts a residential building, open-air car park, fire and medical training centre, Schiphol fire station, immigration and naturalization centre and government agency.

We arrive by bicycle, entering via a small path we have made through the overgrown foliage. At the back of the property is a decaying timber shed. One wall has completely collapsed, leaving only windows suspended in empty space, rotten timber and peeling walls. Walking through the garden stinging nettles brush against our legs.

In between the rear garden shed and main house is another wooden workshop-like space. An industrial workbench with missing drawers sits against the wall opposite large in-built storage racks. The stone floor is covered with leaves, dust and dirt. The whole structure seems waterproof, solid. Three large windows open to face the grey concrete block boundary wall. It is not possible to see either the front or rear road from the workshop.

We begin to set up a place to sleep, laying out black plastic on the stone floor. The main house is only accessible through the back entrance. An old couple used to live here, previously a younger couple with a son. The house was built in 1948. There are holes cut into the floors and walls, randomly scattered throughout the house. The kitchen, living room, bathroom, pantry, entrance hall and sunroom occupy the first floor.

The stone fireplace has collapsed since our last visit. Two bedrooms and a bathroom occupy the second floor. Under the slanted roof are walls covered by striped wallpaper. The wallpaper bubbles in the places it has come unstuck. Mould grows outwards in brown and black rings from where water has leaked through the ceiling.

Pollen rises outside the window. Wearing masks we begin to work, breathing in hot humid air.

[alu-boa]

ⓔ Alumni Event

[001-010]

Feb 2018
Sandberg Instituut
Amsterdam NL

"On Valentines Day, the Studio for Immediate Spaces invites its alumni to the Sandberg for a meet and greet, food and presentations. The aim of the event is not only to meet each other, but to talk about life after Sandberg. Alumni Kristoffer Zeiner Christiansen and Mark Redele will give presentations on post-graduate work, and insights into future hopes and applications for what they had learned in the studio. It is an opportunity for current students to ask questions, and converse about what to expect, how to improve and how to work towards new possibilities within the field of interior architecture — specifically regarding workforce and studio structure."

ⓦ Any Space is the Place

[011-015]

Jan 2019
Sandberg Instituut
Amsterdam NL

By *Jerszy Seymour and Leopold Banchini*
With *The Dirty Art Department, Jurgen Bey and Paulien Bremmer*

"'Space is not only high, it's low. It's a bottomless pit.' *Sun Ra*

The Dirty Art Department presents itself as an open space for all thought, creation and action. It sees itself as a dynamic paradox, flowing between Cecilia Vallejos' notions of *the pure and the applied, the existential and the deterministic, the holy and the profane*. It is concerned with individuality, collectivity and our navigation of the complex relationship between the built world and the natural world, and between other people and ourselves. Although the Dirty Art Department comes from a shared background of design and applied art, it seeks to reject the division between the pure and the applied. Since *God is dead* and *the spectacle* are omnipresent, it sees the creation of alternative and new realities as the way to reconsider our existential situation on this planet.

For one week the SIS and the DAD will design a common space to work, live and create together."

ⓢ At Capacity

[016-025]

Feb 2018
Assembly Hall
Sandberg Instituut
Amsterdam NL

With *Margarita Osipian*

"A group show is a negotiation. At Capacity was a three-day exhibition self-curated by Studio for Immediate Spaces participants in a restricted space. The works produced and displayed were made for the midterm reviews, where the exhibition format was a guideline that participants had to follow. Through the co-production of the exhibition, participants were confronted with questions such as: How does the context of an exhibition shift a work? Further, what delineates or defines a work of art from applied design? What is the language of the work and how does it speak to the public? At Capacity was not only an exercise and task for each individual, but also forced participants into a position of negotiation with each other."

ⓦ Black Out

[026-042]

Dec 2016
DeSchool Club
Amsterdam NL

By *Frédéric Post and Laure Jaffuel*
With *Zoltan Kisák & Dániel Meste, Finder of Things, Madara Délage and the Togetherness, Kees de Haan, Andy Vidal, Valentin Noiret, Pepper Metz & Ivan Cheng, Ibo Ventura & Gaby Vineyard, Very High Tea, Ignas van Rijckevorsel, Orchid, Pipa Collada, Clement Carat and Aurelien Lepetit*

"Shut off the power, unplug the music, switch off the light, the i-Phones, the beer taps, the fridges, the heating, the alarm system ... what else?
Is electricity compulsory in a public place? Or can we switch it off? What does it involve? In security terms, can we find a human alternative, i.e to the smoke detector, instead of relying on technological devices?

When the police intervene in the case of rave parties, they usually pick and seize the electric generator. To which degree are we dependent on electricity in order to party, we, kids of the electronic music?

Black Out is the event organised by Studio for Immediate Space with the artist Frédéric Post, to kick-off the collaboration in between De School and the Sandberg Institute, a series of events and art interventions addressing club culture and late-night parties, curated by Morning Love (Laure Jaffuel and Leila Arenou)."

ⓔ Boarding Ticket

[043-052]

Apr 2018
Ferry Terminal direction NDSM
Central Station
Amsterdam NL

With *Joseph Noonan-Ganley and Tom Vandeputte*

"Beginning at Amsterdam Centraal and traveling north towards NDSM in Amsterdam Noord, the public urban ferry is the stage of a performative reading. Uniformed commuters become the audience of a play on their journey to work. The writing of each participant is presented throughout this trip, where narratives are interwoven with moments of waiting, departure, and arrival."

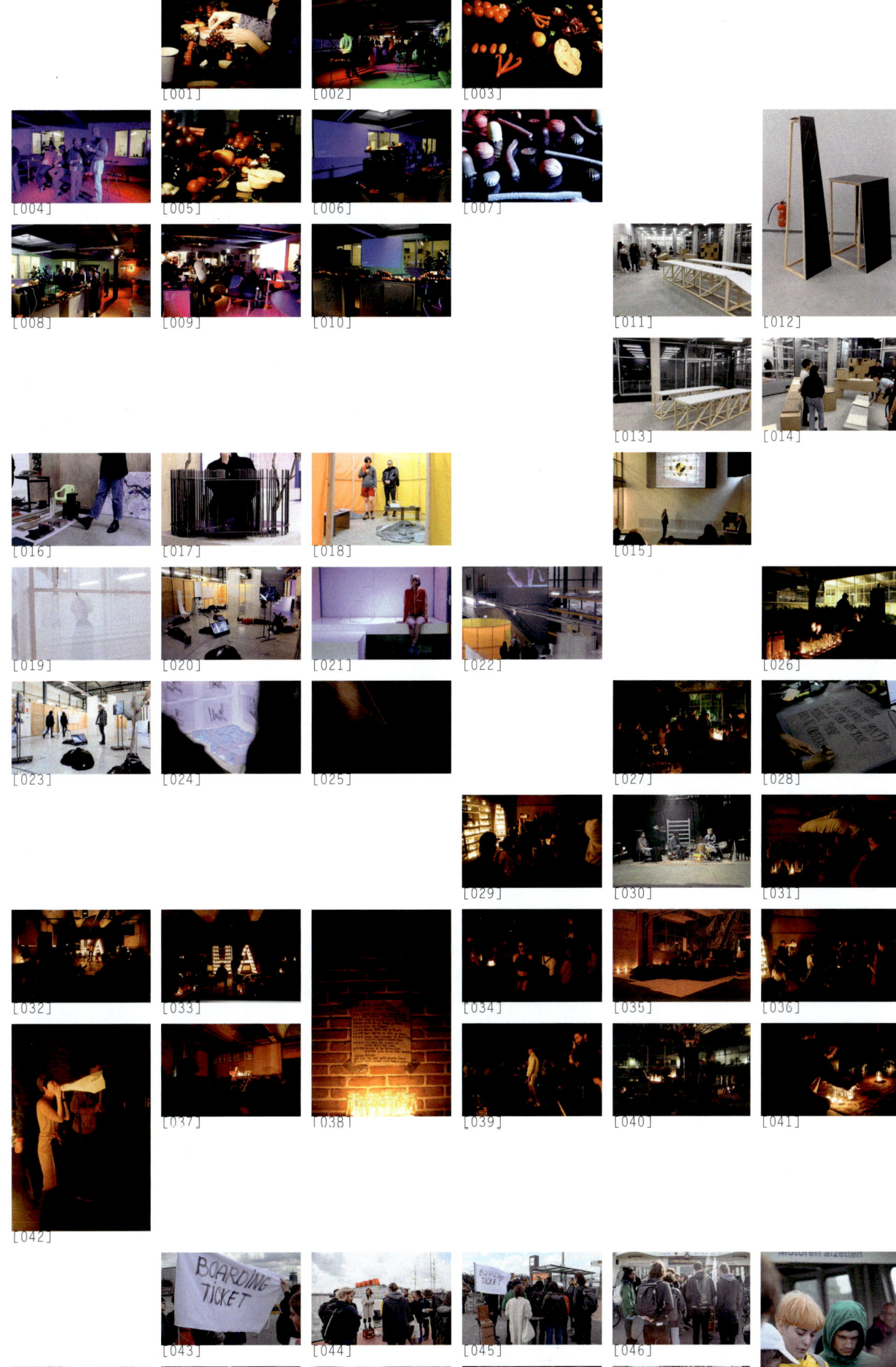

Case Study

[cas-eve]

[053-071]
Dec 2018
Sandberg Instituut
Amsterdam NL

With *Paolo Patelli*

"The Studio for Immediate Spaces affirms that its inspiration and creation finds its source in looking, analysing and understanding existing spaces and contexts. For this show, each participant focuses on researching and analysing a found *immediate* space. By immediate, we mean spaces created by our contemporary culture without the help of professionals. The case study is the base and the inspiration for the projects developed. The tools and methods used for the case study are defined specifically by each participant and discussed with their peers."

Critical Studio

[072-086]
Oct 2017
Sandberg Instituut
Amsterdam NL

By *Lukas Feireiss and Leopold Banchini*
With *The Radical Cut-Up Department, Jurgen Bey and Anne Dessing*

"The Radical Cut-Up Department celebrates the emergence and evolution of the cut-up as the contemporary mode of creativity and dominant global model of cultural production today. *Radical Cut-Up* encourages its participants to copy, combine, create and celebrate experimental forms of creative production.

Against the backdrop of the accelerated growth of new digital technologies that expand the production and circulation of images, text, sound, and objects in contemporary life, the interdisciplinary temporary master thereby draws on a broader definition of the term *cut-up* as a mixture or fusion of disparate elements, or the art of carefully crafted juxtaposition. Within the context of this programme, the term is a container for a long list of names and actions, that describes the mixing and reconfiguration of existing materials to produce new outcomes.

The Studio for Immediate Spaces spent a week together with temporary program *Radical Cut Up*, envisioning, designing and constructing the years' studio spaces for both departments. The aim of the week was to rethink and redesign our workspaces at the Sandberg and to question: How do we work? Further, how can the design of our interior spaces facilitate how we work?"

Event Horizon

Jun 2018
Klaproos
Amsterdam NL

Curation *Boris de Beijer*
With *Rainer Hehl and Julian Schubert*
Text by *Margarita Osipian*

"(Light emitted from inside the event horizon can never reach the outside observer.) And yet, here we are.

The Studio for Immediate Spaces acts as the threshold at which we can encounter space — not as something that is a given — but as something that is constantly being (re)constructed, (re)negotiated, and re(imagined). Those working at this threshold, from a perspective that begins at the intersection of disciplines, aim to give primacy and immediacy to space and disrupt the boundaries and dichotomies often tethered to it.

As a relative concept, an Event Horizon manifests itself differently in relation to an observer and their location. This relativity and relation between the observer and their location, creates the possibility for an infinite number of entrance points into a new and unknown universe, a glimpse of what is yet to come, the shedding of light on what is, always and already, here. As an element of physics, its potential to bend space/time functions as a metaphor for the ongoing slippage between past, present, and future practice.

As a cosmic phenomenon, the Event Horizon signifies the edge of what we can see. In its non-cosmic manifestation, the horizon itself signifies a limit, a boundary, a horizontal connection point between earth and sky. The illusion of its limits, its sharp unwavering divisions, simultaneously embodies a kind of limitlessness. A future that is always on the verge of revealing itself. Always, just slightly, out of reach.

In its more poetic manifestation, an Event Horizon can also be understood as a spherical boundary that can be crossed to enter but cannot be crossed to exit. What then are the boundaries between interiority and exteriority? What happens to information on the threshold of a black hole, in the unknown that is tethered to the edge of the Event Horizon? What emerges in this exhibition is the potential in the unknowable, in the unseeable, in the unimaginable, of what lies beyond the edge."

[087-089]
Domestication
Niels Albers

"A sculpture, born in-between the quest for well designed functional objects and the conflicting tremble of nauseating awareness. A clinical bathroom vibe and tendencies of over-hygienic rooms. Recognisable objects, which have familiarities with bodies from our interiors. Where are we?

Domestication is the process of making a wild animal accustomed to living with or working for humans. Unnecessary suffering, a process invisible to most consumers. Generally, we do not think about the con-sequences of our everyday consumer decisions: decisions that are neither consistent nor rational. Inspired by the highly efficient stainless steel attributes of the slaughter lines, we are presented with captivating objects and seemingly very practical devices. Like a reminiscence of something gone out of order and out of place. Out of time."

[090-092]
20h28 Workshop:
Improvised Spaces
Gauthier Chambry

"Organised as an open platform, *20h28* is a workshop that is focused on gaining a better understanding of improvisation, where spontaneity becomes a way of learning. Using methods and forms of communication of improvised music, dance, rap battles etc, the workshop seeks to question through collective construction/dialogue what improvised spaces can generate and how they affect behavior.

Taking as a starting point of research *la salle polyvalente*, a space provided by the municipality of small french villages, where citizens can organize different kind of events like meetings, weddings, parties, basketball matches, bingo sessions etc; this workshop is focused on the creation of an environment that is shaped by its activity. It is based on two components in perpetual interaction: the material environment of life and the behaviors which it gives rise to and which radically transforms it." *With Arthur Chambry, Quentin Heizmann, Ingeborg Meier Andersern, Luca Salvatori, Zoe Sjollema and Jony Valado*

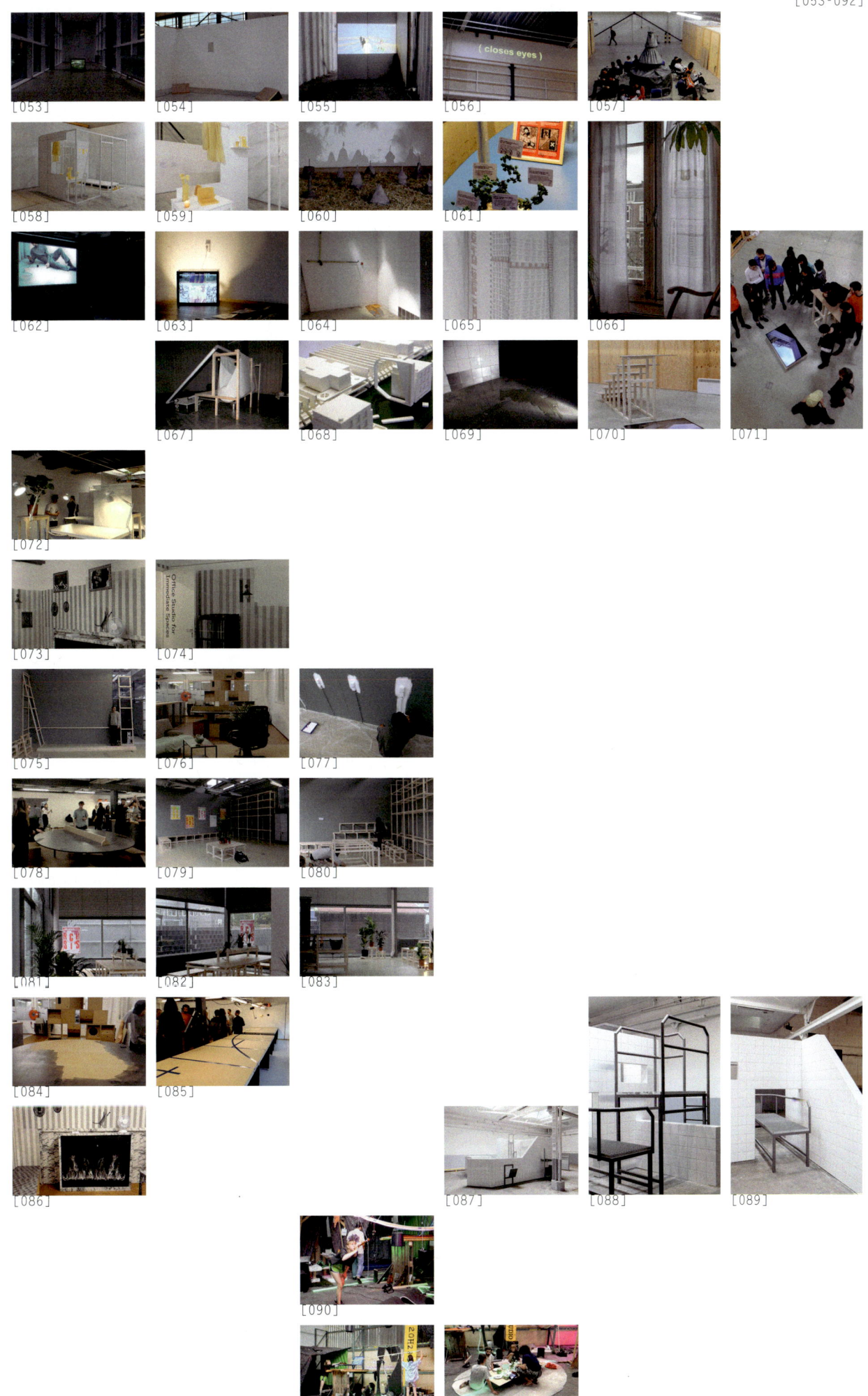

[Event Horizon]

[093-096]
Descending Downwards
Naomi Credé

"And what about voices without bodies and bodies without voices? Are you feeling tired? Drained? Exhausted? It's neither light nor dark outside. The sun is sinking further and further beneath the horizon, accompanied by a looming dullness, as the grey skies gently turn to blackness. Soft blue hues and ambient sound waves fill the room as a bodiless voice close to you speaks out. Let your shoulders relax. Sounds seeping in as you sink into the soft surfaces slumped around you, tired limbs weighing you down. Breath leaking from your lips (be careful not to spill too much). You're here together, congregated and scattered amongst the space whilst other voices are emanating from other parts of the room. Are you feeling comfortable? Calm, soft voices persistently checking up on your wellbeing. Remember to remain composed and in control. Their voices don't grow tired like yours. Did the darkness descend suddenly? Or did darkness fall upon you slowly?" *Music by Andreas Tegnander*

[098-100]
Encampment of other Spaces
Samuel Kuhfuss Gustavsen

"The cluster-like life-size model stems from the idea of depicting life in juxtaposed spaces that show an imaginary world that viewers can visit, invoking the presence of a twenty first century hermit who has escaped to a temporary dwelling. The idea of a diorama as an architectural portal — a gate into a new way of creating scenarios for a human to divide, define, conceal and control the access to their present settings. The structures want to evoke an entirely fictional and imaginary universe, dissolving boundaries between mental spaces and built surroundings and the landscape in which it is situated. When museums are less about artifacts or the institution itself, but they really become more about narratives. Like the taxidermist, whose work is deeply marked by human longing and the inanimate taken from the animate world and posed into the speculative diorama format, that is shaped and are shaping our relationship with the natural world."

[101-103]
Jelly Coasts and Milk Rivers
Liene Pavloska

"*Jelly Coasts and Milk Rivers* is an expression used in the Latvian language when describing a fictional place of wealth and happiness. Growing up in Latvia, where society shifted from a communist past towards a capitalist future, I wonder how hope is represented in these regimes and how narratives of the past and present are created, while directed and played out within the Urban Stage. While working I looked into a comparison between city planning and the creation of theater performance. Peter Brook in The Empty Space describes Deadly and Immediate Theatre. Deadly Theatre — meaning theatre that is trapped in tradition and repetition, the kind that approaches classics from the viewpoint that somewhere, some-one has found out how the play should be done and Immediate Theatre — meaning theatre that is responsive towards the here and now. I wonder what would happen if one appreciates the performative aspect of daily life and appropriates the awareness of performa-tivity? Talking about Deadly Theatre Peter Brook states: 'When we say deadly, we never mean dead: we mean something depressingly active, but for this very reason capable of change.'" *With Mathilde Stubmark and Elisabeth Mesnier*

[104-107]
TBD
Mirko Podkowik

"*TBD* contemplates the status of work and its current and prospective transformation. The common notioris of this term have changed and are being constantly re-evaluated. What constitutes work today and who is a worker? If the fantasy of a fully automated world becomes a reality, what to do with our own hands? When some economies turn away from physical goods, targeting human attention, those commercial relationships become as immaterial as human relationships always have been. We become managers of our net-works of relations, that slip in and out of commercial nature. Promoting ourselves exposes the mode we engage with the world now — polishing our self-image for social and economic relationships, and at the same time surrendering to the neo-liberal idea of profit and maximizing value. *TBD* shows cliche scenes that appear inevitably important to the protagonist and the viewer alike, but are really just hollow, meaningless actions. Work, only existent to be executed."

[108-111]
The Garden of (Un)/ Becoming
Malissa Anne Canez Sabus

"*The Garden of (Un)/Becoming* works with/in the borders of cultivated space and spaces of wilderness, interiorities/exteriorities, in the space of carriance. It is interested in the notion of relational architecture, an architecture whose dynamic structures not only frame, but also transmit and receive; threading and nourishing multiple realities individually and collectively through the mode of carrying. It is interested in gardening as an architectural methodology, where time and duration contingently unfold, where the basis of practice is grounded in care for what already is, and what is to come; a methodology where space is never empty but rather living and thriving and constantly in motion. It uses the wasteland/meadow as its foundation; the marginal space where nature/culture co-emerge into a living reality. Such space is used as a platform for reframing human/earth relations, looking at notions of control, value, productivity, nour-ishment and the potential for landscapes of alterity within the context of the urban fabric."

[112-114]
Unconditional Void
Rein Verhoef

"An abandoned thing found alongside the road, initially it carried a void in it that appealed to me. It caught my attention because of all the qualities yet to be discovered in these supports.
    By physically working fanatically on these objects and slightly changing their initial characteristics, they became monumental bodies on their own. The process of repeating this shape evoked an undisturbed static emptiness. Leftovers of a production process that had found a new potential value in my way of constructing their own space. Monumental bodies have infiltrated space temporarily. These objects are objects of display. They will define their position towards each other. Where the round is positioned against the square and the oval against the rectangle. Where these four became silent covenants. An elementary juxtaposition."

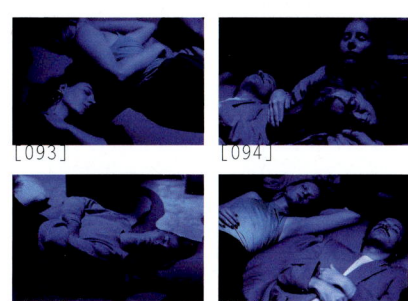

[093] [094] [095] [096]

[097] [098] [099]

[100]

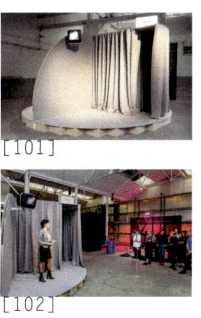

[101] [102]

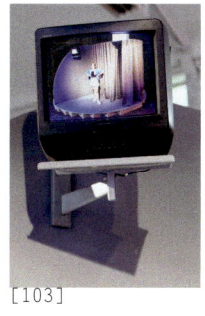

[103]

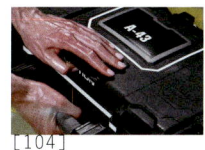

[104]

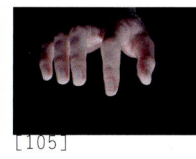

[105]

[106]

[107]

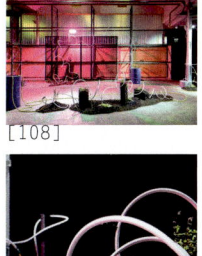

[108]

[109]

[110] [111]

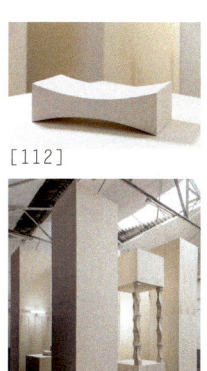

[112] [114]

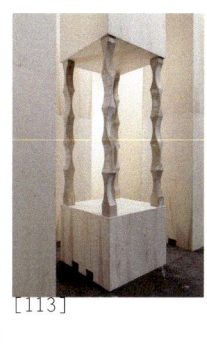

[113]

[fab-gre]

● Fabulous Future

```
[FF01]   Are We There Yet? 2019
[FF02]   The Ascending Hour 2019
[FF03]   Fabulous Future 2109
[FF04]   Are We There Yet? 2019
[FF05]   The Ascending Hour 2019
[FF06]   Don't You Ever Go 2019
[FF07]   Welcome to GEL 2018
[FF08]   PUBcast Station 2019
[FF09]   Soft Opening 2018
[FF10]   White Nights 2018
[FF11]   PUBcast Station 2019
[FF12]   Clearescent Green 2019
[FF13]   The Ascending Hour 2019
[FF14]   Soft Opening 2018
[FF15]   White Nights 2018
[FF16]   Clearescent Green 2019
[FF17]   Clearescent Green 2019
[FF18]   Don't You Ever Go 2019
[FF19]   Soft Opening 2018
[FF20]   Clearescent Green 2019
```

Fabulous Future is a collective of seven and an ongoing project which formed after graduating together from Studio for Immediate Spaces, Sandberg Instituut. It is a project which binds together research, development and the construction of spaces, events and situations.

Fabulous Future is committed to an expanded notion of space making, and flourishes from a broad range of backgrounds and skills: fine arts, design, architecture, scenography, cooking, woodworking, writing, gardening, sound, video, performance, etc. The methodology of the collective revolves around continual negotiation in order to reach a shared outcome and encompasses constant consideration of surrounding social and political contexts. This form of work and self-organisation allows projects to have a unique means of process-led and critical production; inclusive to expanded notions of everyday rituals (being together, cooking, sleeping, dancing and caring for each other), which are an integral part of *Fabulous Future*.

ⓦ The Fabric of Sound

[115-121]

May 2017
Sandberg Instituut
Amsterdam NL

By Matt Stokes

"The sounds around us can have a significant impact on our psychology. For good or bad, auditory stimuli can influence our emotions, and thinking ability. Sound can alter our perception of the things around us, and affect our productivity. The difference between perceiving *sound* and *noise*, has much to do with desire and meaning, and depends, in part, on who you are and what you've experienced in life.

Most of us are often unbothered by the presence of certain sounds, whereas noise is unwanted sound. It can alter performance, satisfaction, health or concentration making it relevant to almost every setting from learning environments, offices, industrial buildings to modes of transit, homes, neighbourhoods and hospitals. However, loud, continuous, and cacophonous noise can also be experienced positively, depending on the social context.

Music deeply connects with this and is often linked to memories that can instantly change the mood you're in, depending on whether (and how) it reminds you of good times or bad. A psychologist writing about connections between Electronic Dance Music and well-being describes her first memorable encounter with the music: "Considering that I was surrounded by people much older than me, in an abandoned warehouse, in the middle of nowhere ... I felt safe. My brother disappeared into the crowd shortly after he positioned me in front of the speakers, and I spent the rest of the night dancing and watching the people around me ... They all shared a love of music, and a primal need to dance. For a 13-year-old girl who wasn't very popular at school, the fact that I was in a place that I felt so welcomed, despite being clearly *different*, changed my life." This story could be true for anyone's first experience of any other genre of music.

The sound system plays a pivotal role in the person's experience quoted. Its design has the ability to pump out sound that is not only heard, but also physically felt, stimulating activities of the parts of the brain that regulate emotion and vital functions such as heart rate and breathing. If everyone who congregates around a sound system is immersed in and feeling something on a par with each other, both the individual and collective experience can be powerful.

The history of sound system culture largely begins in post-war developments in the Jamaican music scene. Rapidly, its influence spread further afield, often amongst immigrant communities, before becoming part of a wider creative scene that has aided the birth of significant social and cultural phenomenon, as well as weaving itself into the re-writing of public law enforcement.

The workshop will explore the design, historical and socio-political nature of sound systems alongside the ability of sound and music to transform space, the individual and community. A key part of the workshop will focus on building and testing a functioning sound system that has the potential to be used in or outside the Instituut."

Ⓢ Green Light

[123-132]

April 2018
Amsterdam NL

With Jerszy Seymour and Jurgen Bey

"Other than what we can produce materially (what we can design and build), a situation is a set of conditions, rather than a formal outcome.

It's a moment, produced in both space and time, ranging across material, social, political and economic relations. Events; occurring, intended, by accident, gotten out of hand, daily, spectacular — situations are everywhere, which makes it challenging to define what it is as a practice.

The practice of *space* exceeds any formal definition of it (the theory, the model) because it revolves around the experience of it (here, now). Then, relating it to the architectural field, is like putting the gears in reverse: space exists because we occupy it. In that sense, it does not rely on design (the plan, the image), but on the potential of design (the effect, transcendence).

If you want to dance, you don't have to build a dancefloor: you just have to dance."

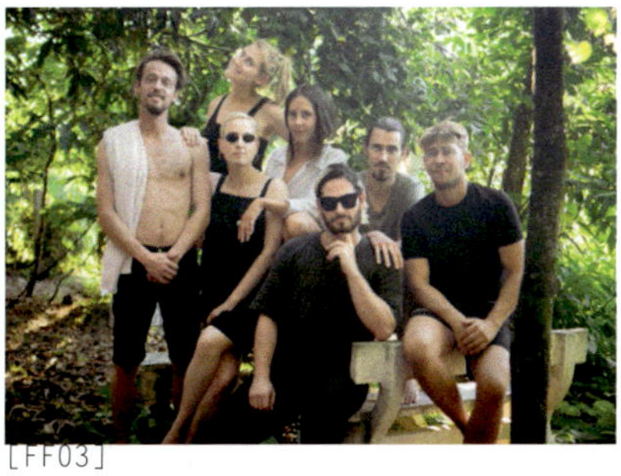
[FF03]

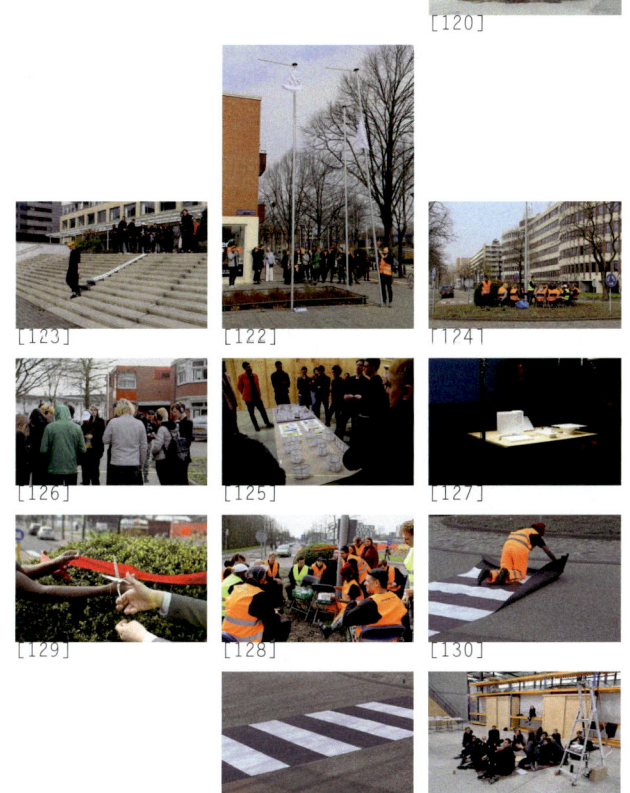

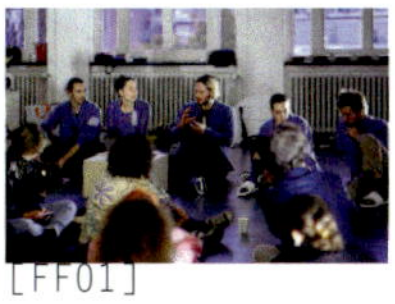
[FF01]

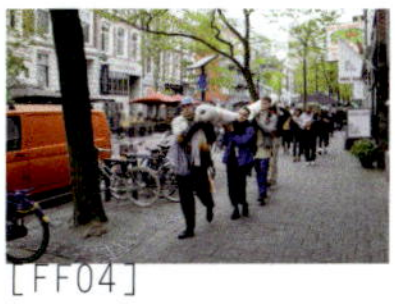
[FF04]

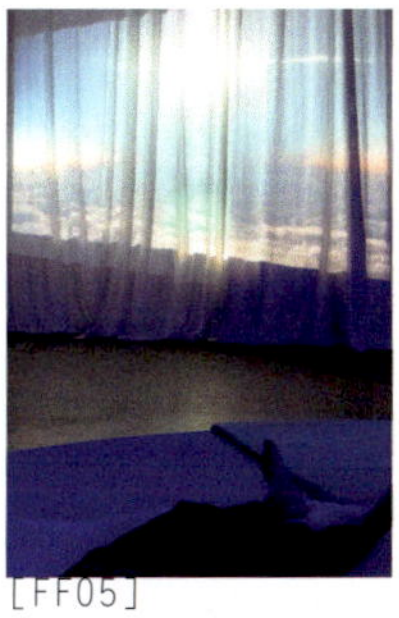
[FF05]

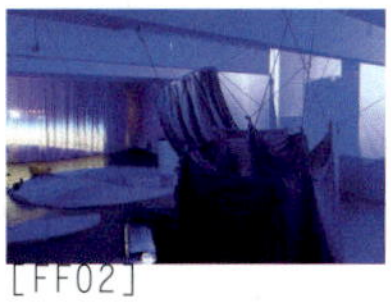
[FF02]

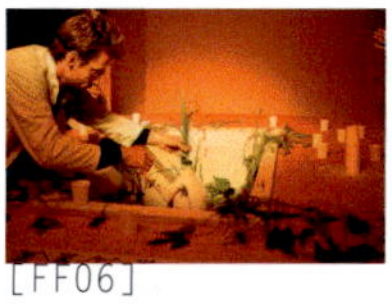
[FF06]

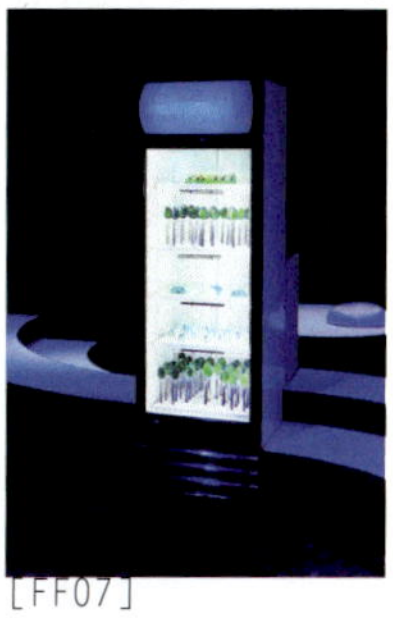
[FF07]

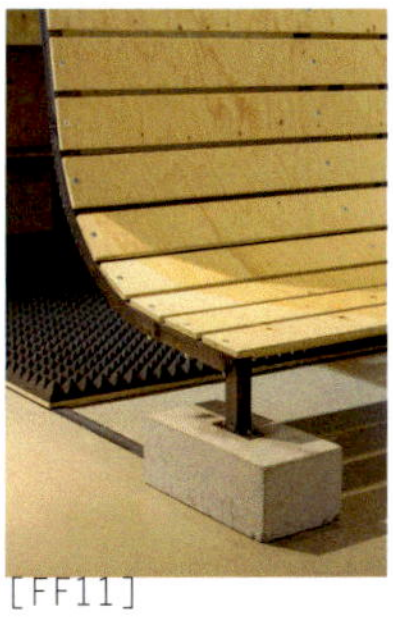
[FF11]

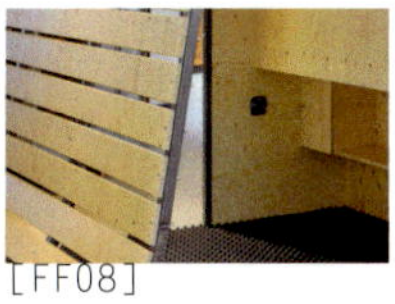
[FF08]

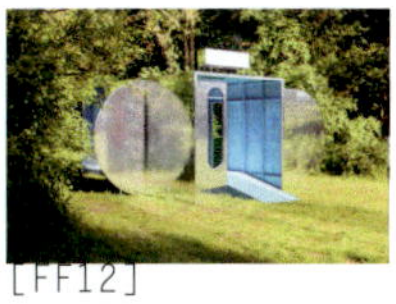
[FF12]

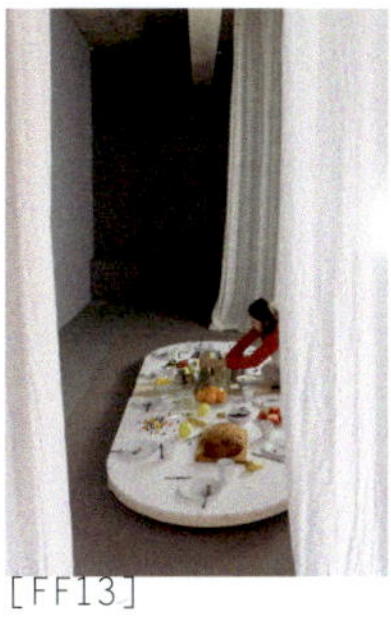
[FF13]

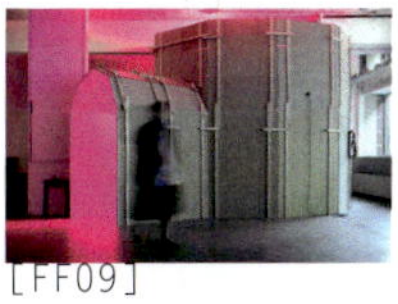
[FF09]

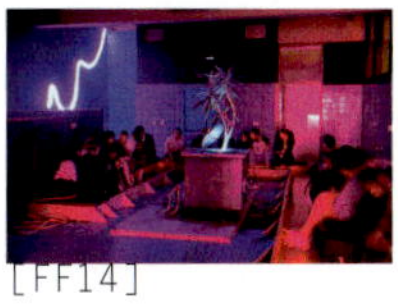
[FF14]

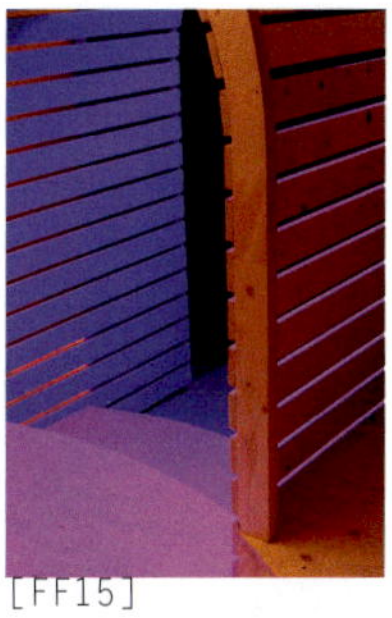
[FF15]

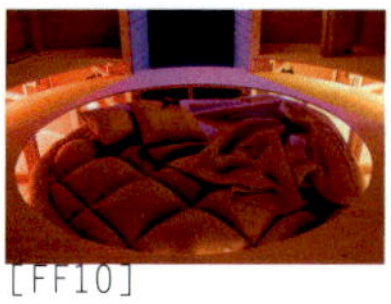
[FF10]

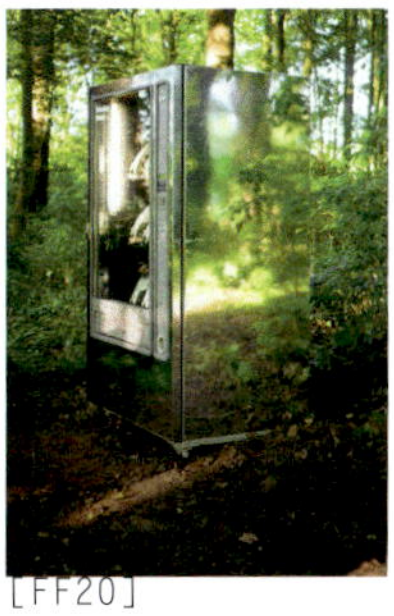
[FF20]

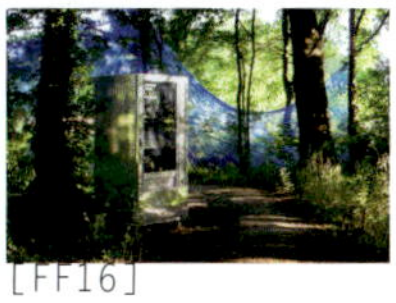
[FF16]

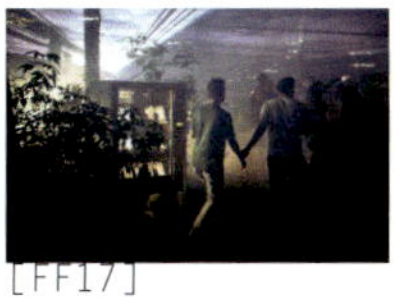
[FF17]

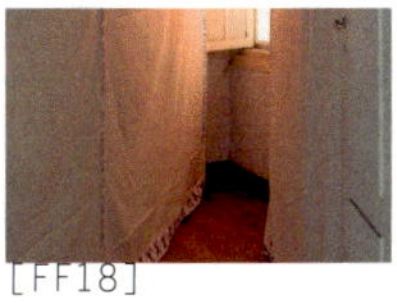
[FF18]

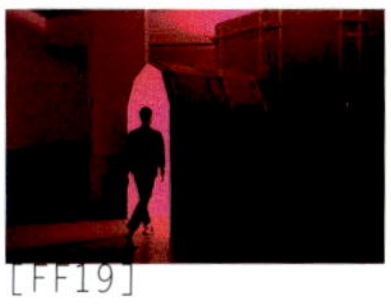
[FF19]

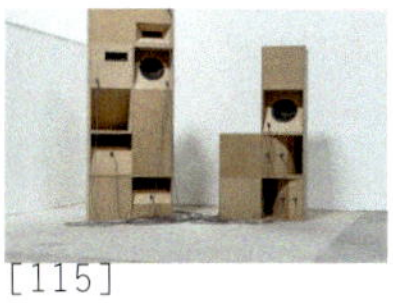
[115]

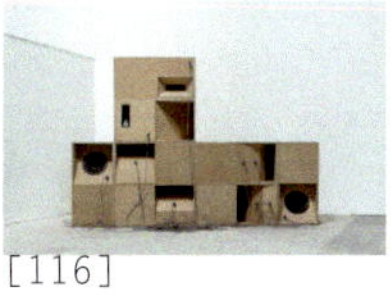
[116]

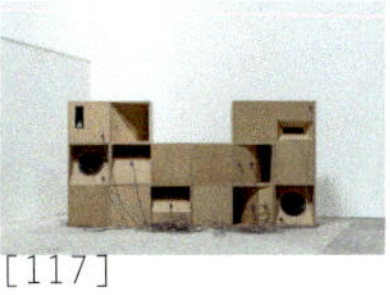
[117]

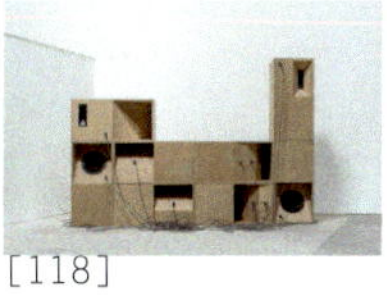
[118]

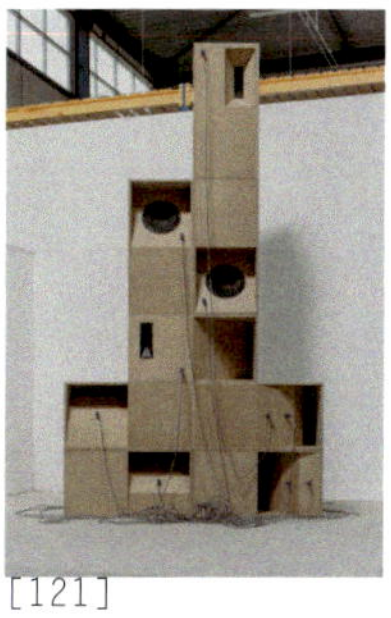
[121]

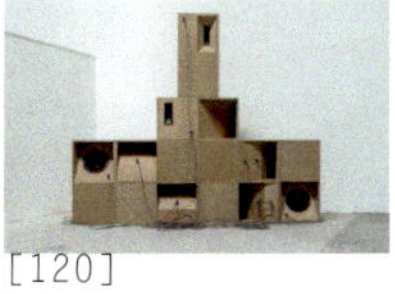
[120]

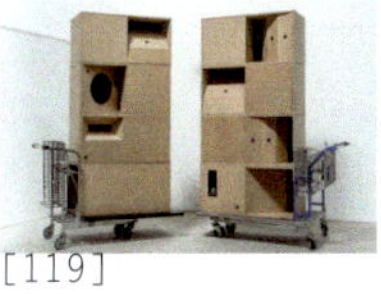
[119]

[122]

[123]

[124]

[126]

[125]

[127]

[129]

[128]

[130]

[131]

[132]

[hou-in]

ⓢ The House

[133-158]

Jun 2018
Schipol NL

With *Mark Minkjan*

"Empty space is a rarity in Amsterdam. Buildings lean exhausted against one another. The House is the culmination of one year of individual and collaborative work. A communal living experience, we, the participants of the first year of Studio for Immediate Spaces, spent five days inhabiting a vacant house located on the outskirts of Amsterdam. The house stood within the territory of Schiphol Airport in a restricted area. Consequently, we developed specific strategies for accessing, moving through and occupying the house. Responding to the house, the context and the immediate needs of living, we established spatial programs negotiating how to create and live together discreetly. We wished to question the form of a traditional exhibition, the difficulty of finding space in Amsterdam and what it means to temporarily occupy an abandoned plot of land in a sensitive context. The police entered the property after being made aware of our presence through noise complaints. We were given a warning, told to leave immediately and our identities were recorded."

ⓦ In Progress

[159-191]

May 2019
Sao Miguel
Azores PT

By *Hector Zamora*
With *Jesse James, Luis Brum, Sofia Carolina Botelho, João Rebelo Costa and Walk and Talk Festival*

"In Progress is a workshop where I will share the strategies that I follow to develop a site-specific artwork for a new and unknown context. Far from theory, we will work together to create the experience of a site visit in São Miguel. Perhaps the site visit can become an artwork itself ...

When an exhibition commissions me to develop a site specific artwork, I start with a program for the site; a site visit, a timeline for work and the end goal of opening day.

The schedule of the site visit will work as the structure and goal of the site visit, but it doesn't mean that the schedule is not fluid and flexible according to the real experiences to be had.

Ideas can find the perfect spot to grow and materialise hybrid or entirely new ideas inspired by the visit. With good luck, you can arrive at something during the site visit, if not you have to continue in your studio. For that reason it is important to see, touch, smell, feel, talk, hear, test, try, do, walk, drive, eat, drink, live ... as much as possible.

The way to keep all this information depends on your own strategies that can go from photos, films, drawings, notes, sound records ..."

[in]

In the Open

[192-194]

Jun 2019
Van Ostadestraat
Amsterdam NL

Curation *Elise van Mourik and Laure Jaffuel*
With *Yana Foqué, Ludwig Engel and De Fabriek Volkskamer*

"Taking place in the public domain of a dense city street in the centre of Amsterdam, *In the Open* addresses the fluidity of public space, unfolding as time-piece over the course of three days including performances, objects, interventions, films, spaces and situations produced by the 2019 graduates of the Studio for Immediate Spaces.

In the Open reflects on public space as a space that continually undergoes transformation, compelled by changing relationships between economic, cultural and socio-political interests. Public space is a space of negotiation. Between individuals and a sense of place, government policy and the common good or corporate enterprise and its exposure to the world as a market. Public space is both a community's most inner place, where those interests belong and inhabit, in real time — and its outer-outside, a surface of competing idea's, of communication strategy, where images are produced or maintained, in ideal time. Public space is both life and story, in no particular order. We've asked ourselves "What makes something public?", and found it overwhelmingly definition-fluid; some spaces are open to all but not accessible to all, some situations are for free but do not produce equal liberties in terms of gender, race, social background, ... — *public* is a fluid term, especially in times where the economic, the social, and the political freely flow into one another. The Open floor plan of the neoliberal project, the jungle of the Enterprise-become-landscape. Thinking of publicness brings into question the open, the authentic, the planned, the autonomous, the common, the fluent — it demands a relational perspective, which is at the core of this exhibition. Taking place as an open scenario *In the Open* will reflect on how audiences and publics are addressed, dealing with subjects such as housing, community and fiction, alternative economies, social capital, individualisation, space and gender, urban space and intimacy, to reflect on publicness as a situation of exchange, a relationship, and its many forms and implications."

[195-197]
Unreal Estates:
The Tale of Liberty Hills
Andrea Belosi

"*Unreal Estates: The Tale of Liberty Hills* is a CGI short film that employs — and exploits — the media of architectural renderings as virtual sets for a fictional narrative. *From the city to the countryside*, the contemporary tendency promoted as life solution, is the leitmotif of the story of the protagonist. Exhausted by the struggle for entrepreneurial success, he sets off to the countryside. Like a mirage, a bright landscape appears on the horizon — and it fades away in the blink of an eye." *Graphics by Bin Koh*

[198-201]
As the cupboard is to the home,
so the home is to the cupboard
Elia Castino

"The work expands from a research on domesticity, focusing on the living conditions of international students in the city of Amsterdam. In a context where housing struggle is rampant, the project looks at real occurrences to reflect upon the way domestic daily life unfolds. When the conventional structure of the house *evaporates* new forms are generated; the architecture for the home becomes scattered, hybrid, ephemeral, a series of habits, rituals and routines, a simple pure moment in space."

[202-205]
Commoning the Bread
Antoine Guay

"The urban context affects collective organizations and common interests by promoting individual ways of living. Cities like Amsterdam are the main players within this logic of transformation and show it in their urban landscapes. Within these, construction dumpsters become the markers of this shift. *Commoning the Bread* proposes to turn a dumpster into a communal bread oven. It aims to explore the potentialities of resistance through a creative alternative by disrupting the urban context." *Special thanks to Jony Valado*

[206-209]
Chei del fouc
Francesca Lucchitta

"*Chei del Fouc* is a fictional community suspended between experience, desire and imagination. They are living in the mountain environment of the Alps and are the result of moments of contact with different communities and ways of relating to a mountain environment. They existed in the past, are existing in the present and will probably exist in the future. They represent a parallel way of living in relation to that of the people living in the city, far away from nature."

[210-212]
Capillary Malformation
Davide-Christelle Sanvee

"*Capillary Malformation* is a site-specific audio walk that moves between different spaces and times, interweaving fiction and reality. Drawing on feminist science fiction books, architectural theory and lived experiences, the listener is faced with the gendered nature of domestic spaces." *Special thanks to Mina Young Pedersen, Ali Glover, Francesca Lucchitta*

[213-215]
Everything around,
including you
Maike Statz

"The work integrates itself in the dailylife's routine by using its social codes and existing architecture. Engaged with topics touching the relations between individuals and their positionality in public spaces, she proposes a scripted performance that assume its intention: to perturbate in order to requestion our behaviors. By initiating a situation where the street's occupants have to negotiate with each others, she wants to challenge the expectations of her audience."

[216-218]
Heterogenous Waters
Elizaveta Strakhova

"*Heterogeneous Waters* is a communal bathing experience that takes place in a public foot bath. The work addresses the consequences of the increasing privatisation of the rituals of self-care and hygiene. Through the re-introduction of the disappearing public bathing facilities into the urban fabric it explores their potential for stimulating the development of scenarios for care, inclusion and intimacy within the public realm."

[219-221]
Secure, Peaceful & Wild
Mathilde Stubmark

"The project investigates how humans sense of smell relates to space. In contrary to commonly used methods of designing architectural entities, scent is the main protagonist in the process of space making. *Secure, Peaceful & Wild* is a research on how scents can be incorporated into materials recognized from the world of architecture, such as plaster, concrete, ceramics or textiles. The manipulated materials are spatially examined to understand the possible affect on the human body and mind."

[193]

[192]

[194]

[195]

[196]

[197]

[198]

[199]

[200]

[201]

[203]

[202]

[204]

[205]

[206]

[207]

[209]
[208]

[210]

[211]

[212]

[213]

[214]
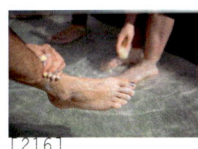
[216]

[217]

[218]

[215]

[219]

[220]

[221]

Infrastructure of Intimacy

[222-225]

Mar 2018
Noord-Zuid metro line
Amsterdam NL

By Bas Hendrikx and Gieneke Pieterse
With Lara Almarcegui, Femke Herregraven and Samantha Thole

"The infrastructure for transport is the starting point, in this case, the metro. Amsterdam is developing the Noord Zuid lijn: it connects the wealthiest part of the city (Zuidas) with one of the poorest parts (Buikslotermeer in Noord) and helps to increase living conditions in the area as well as support gentrification processes. We don't want to take that too literally, but instead, want to explore with the students how to break with binary oppositions in architecture. For instance, many people generally consider architecture as very masculine, whereas being enclosed in a space is somehow also very feminine. For the methodology week we want to look at gender in architecture, and let the students make proposals for *queering* architecture and infrastructure. That means we will look at how the spaces of public transport are (unintendedly?) designed for the hetero normativity and the patriarchy. Feminist scholar Susan Leigh Star, has described the *infrastructural turn* as: "an embedded strangeness, a second-order one, that of the forgotten, the background, the frozen in place".

We will ask the students to make a work, a performance or an intervention that will take place by the end of the week on Friday evening in an Amsterdam metro or metro station. It will be unannounced to the authorities. The aim is to make a work or a proposal in which they play with perception of the space of the metro. The mobility of dynamics of a moving public space with the fluidity of a queer approach. Their work should undermine the power play in the designed spaces of the metro, transforming the public transport system into something inclusive and inviting to all."

Instant Composition

[226-237]

Nov 2018
Extra City
Antwerpen BE

By Margaux Amoros and Cecile Brousse
With Elise van Mourik, Christine Roggeman and Esther Genicot

"An instant composition of spaces dialoguing with dance. Performing bodies and scenography acting on each other and revealing each other. *Instant composition* is about creating pieces with no score. Choreography-scenography happens as events are taking place under the eye of the audience. You will explore how to produce performing material spontaneously together with the dancers/musicians and refine the compositional aspects of the collective creativity.

In our improvisation work we are deeply interested in the atmosphere of the flight and its special *near future timing*. It is important for us to practice alertness and we maintain attention to the situation so that we are always able to run away from it, to transform it.

Like children, we love to invent, destroy and continuously re-invent.
Let's get physical
Let's get sharp
Let's get better
Let's eat something
The show must go on."

Jam

[238-246]

Feb 2017
Never Neverland
Amsterdam NL

With Dieter Dietz

"Ascetic memory plan habits databank miniaturisation tailor from screen to street long-term strategies adapting everyday jewelry, back and forth, smell light the audience turns filtered remodeling the basic a lot of things happening starts and ends with a space."

Jojo's Bizaare Adventure

[247-255]

May 2017
Kas Keerweer
Amsterdam NL

With Joseph Noonan-Ganley and Tom Vandeputte

"*Jojo's Bizarre Adventure* is a public reading event located at Kas Keerweer greenhouse in Amsterdam. The event consists of a shared meal and performative readings in which students speak their own and each other's texts, blurring the boundaries between voice, style and content."

[222-255]

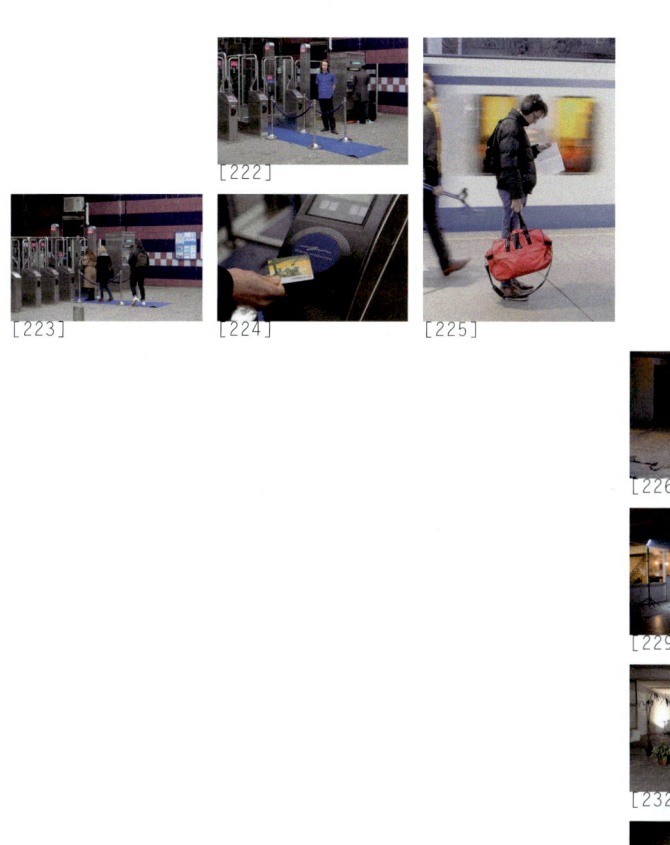

149

Lesbos Falafel

[256-261]
Jan 2016
Mytilini
Lesbos GR

With   *No Border Kitchen Mytilini, Leopold Banchini, Pierre Cauderay, Silvia Converso, Louis Mejean, Jeremy Schuh, Jacopo Porsini, Luísa Pires and others*

"*Lesbos Falafel* was a temporary action set in Lesbos together with No Border Kitchen. No Border Kitchen Lesbos is a long lasting self-organised group of individuals who maintain a solidarity structure on the Greek Island of Lesbos. The main purpose of the collective is to support travellers who are unable to progress with their journey due to European migratory policies. Through a praxis based on mutual aid and solidarity, it takes a stand against border policies and the suffering they are causing. Providing basic needs, NBK is trying to offer a viable alternative to the way travellers are treated by mainstream NGO's, governments, and local authorities, which is often characterised by condescension, coupled with a dehumanising and infantilising attitude.

This adventure, organised not long before the start of *No Border Calais*, layed the fundamental concepts behind our teaching at the Sandberg Institute."

Material Gesture

[262-274]
Nov 2017
NL, BE

By   *Remco Siebring*
With   *Kemner Foundry, Hainaut Quarries, Dutch National Opera, 3D Print Canal House, Van Tetterode Glass Studio and Brick Factory Rodruza*

"As creatives, how we make often depends on which materials we choose for our works. *Places of Production* is a workshop aimed to introduce and familiarise participants with various materials and potential material gestures. To question whether these gestures can redefine ways of making and constructing. What are the gestures that give shape to the environments we inhabit? What is the correlation between material and craft? What places of production can be utilized for future collaboration within our local region, and how, on a practical level can this be executed?"

Monument to my Mother

[275-276]
Feb 2017
Amsterdam NL

By   *Simon Fujiwara*

"The purpose of this workshop is to create a *Monument to your Mother*. There are very few days to execute the project, so the monument will and should reflect the nature of the time limit, and can be presented in any form you wish as long as you can communicate verbally and/or visually the monument to the class in a five-minute presentation. The form of the presentation can take any form, from projection, lecture, pitch, guided tour, architectural intervention, drawings, music or sound, images only, short story, physical spatial performance, video, as long as it is only five minutes long and is presented live.

The brief is open to be interpreted as you wish as long as whatever you present engages with the idea of a monument and argues its relation to physical context and the individual represented. You are encouraged to think as broadly and fluidly as you can about this project, engaging with ideas of time, history, individual, public space, economy, urbanism, architecture, performance, identity, abstraction, representation and the conflict between ideology and reality."

Nagele by Nagele

[277-287]
Mar 2019
Nagele NL

By   *Katinka de Jonge*
With   *Céline Talens and Jurgen Bey*

"Does the Western Modernist idea of the Tabula Rasa still exist? How can we look to a village like Nagele with eyes of 2019?

In a time of enormous social and ecological change, the modernist idea of the New Town may sound odd, or just completely illusory. If there is one thing the impact of human presence and action has shown us, is that the earth is one huge ecosystem and everything is inevitably related to everything. Simultaneously, calibrated idea's on colonisation in parts of the world as being *new empty land* are unmasked one after the other, we cannot ignore that our nature, as well as our culture, is completely interwoven with familiar and alien history and a (collective) feeling of belonging and/or estrangement.

In reaction to this, old power structures are questioned and more people believe in *collective bottom-up* organisational strategies, this can go from collective caretaking, education to housing. Design is seen as something participatory rather than a determinative system. But a lot of material and immaterial structures in our society do not move that easily, so we are forced to use the existing in search for a new formula. Or maybe it should not even become a formula. Nor a plan.

The question is: How can we experience Modernist ruins from below, looking up instead of looking over a map, and how then, do we to discover the holes, the cracks, the ruptures, from which we are able to re-interpret, re-build, re-learn, re-vision and re-late?"

[256-287]

[new]

ⓖ New Town

[288-290]

Jun 2017
Station Noord
Amsterdam NL

Curation *Bas Hendrix*
With *Julian Schubert, Andrea Rodriguez Novoa and Joel Vacheron*
"The unwritten laws of urban planning predict that a metro station is never misplaced and will always become a centre, regardless of its location. Unlike train stations metro stops have the ability to create social space around infrastructure. In *New Town*, that notion becomes a metaphor to address urban expansion, dwelling in transition and the artificiality of constructed space. Taking place in a completed yet vacant metro station in Amsterdam's Noord/Zuidlijn, the space hosts the projects of 13 artists, architects and designers. New Town explores the potentiality of space. Whether physical or virtual, *New Town* is a site for prospects with regard to space. Exploring such topics as identity and space, the works in this exhibition depart from cultural, personal and historical accounts, oftentimes bordering between fact, fiction and constructed realities. *New Town* is the 2017 graduation exhibition of Studio for Immediate Spaces and will be accompanied by performances, gastronomy and events."

[291-293]
I am Therefore
Nadjim Bigou

"Technological advancements increasingly dilute the limit between human and machine: Nadjim Bigou believes the notion of the Makina Sociabilis seems highly conceivable. The annihilation of subject and object would be then an unavoidable question that mankind will have to deal with. Would objects become subjects? Or could it be humans that would become objects?"

[294-295]
Drive-In Landscape
Hein van Duppen

"*Drive-in Landscape* is a décor for a photo-shoot, set in a canyon landscape. Visitors are invited to drive their car into the artificial setting and have their photograph taken. The installation depicts the car frozen in action with the driver behind the steering wheel. The work embodies and comments on the constructed commercial dream of the car as object of freedom and mobility. *Drive-in-Landscape* evokes the car's promise of spectacular journeys into mountains, metropolitan centres, deserts, forests and seasides. The landscape props, camera, flashlight, the photographer, the hosts, the driver and the car together stage a situation that forms a performative act."

[296-300]
DMM
Arie de Fijter

"*DMM* is a collection of abstract models whose appearance lean towards domestic furniture. Slab, Stack, Crust and Plateau refer to notional landscapes that are situated beyond the furniture itself. They embody two working methods that correlate with dualistic dispositions. First is corporeal; a cast taken from the traced trepidation of a body defines an imaginary topography. Second performance in collaboration with Ksenia Perek is computerized; controlled duplication of archetypal shapes introduces overarching aqueducts and skyward spiral stairs. The combination of both are read as an architectural allegory of vulnerability and persistence, wherein each object claims specific scale and position. The installation is modular. Performance conducts the narrative from monumental and ceremonial composures towards fragmented derangements. Throughout this journey, bodies perform similar dualities as the fetishes they manipulate." *With Ksenia Perek*

[301-304]
Else Here (Process as Station)
Carolin Gießner

"Interested in our being together in space — a place that is made by action — Carolin Gießner has created a site-specific installation that is displaced throughout the exhibition and beyond. The diachronistic plots unfold to the beholder like scenes of a play. The character of the metro station as a hub for people in transit leads the way for the meandering of her works throughout the architecture. A station is a place you go to to go somewhere else. Exploring the *madeness* of our reality Gießner skews familiar objects into materialized fictions. Within her work she employs tactile tactics to move through (non)-physical matters that allow the work to be developed in close relation to the specific context in which they are experienced. She is interested in devising sites of togetherness that allows for third spaces to emerge: an approach that requires a continuous balancing of all elements at play."

[305-307]
Making a Living
Eva Hoonhut

"For almost a year Hoonhout has been focused on furniture as a frame to engage with systems of production. As well as this she has found different ways to engage with the bodily movements and traces of habits within our daily existence. In *Making a Living* Hoonhout produced a sculptural situation that opens up a reflection around the constructed nature of a private space, a home, and the narrative imposed by mass production. By using the character of the commercial window display and different points of view from the *inside-and-outside*, she sets up a narration that deals with the depicted new object and the active used object. On different levels the work deals with the value of the physical, the material and the image. It questions authenticity and our physical connection to our own living spaces. Wooden objects with print, ceramic glazed objects, carpet, fabric, plastic, ready made objects (chairs, shoes, lamps)."

[308-313]
Hero's Banquet
Shih-Hui Hung

"This event *The Hero's Banquet* was inspired by the scenes and settings encountered along the journey undertaken by Shih-Hui Hung whilst creating the comic TWAT. Each piece depicts the effect of entropy over time in three and two dimensions, respectively. This process of energy dissipation and transformation provide the driving force of the Wheel of Life, the structural symbol upon which the archetypal hero's journey is mapped."
With Malissa Canez-Sabus, Ting Gong, Ivan Cheng, Rixta van der Molen and Jonathan Mehrez

[314-318]
We stare series
Lily Lanfermeijer

"In December 2016, Lily Lanfermeijer travelled to Andhra Pradesh, India to create new work. Lanfermeijer focuses on the fabric trade between India and The Netherlands during the VOC period. In The Netherlands, these fabrics were seen as exotic and subsequently used and reproduced in different techniques like embroidery in Dutch traditional attire. For this installation, original patterns found in the printers' workshops were adjusted and remixed with western architectural and modernist influences. Lanfermeijer questions the role of authorship within the context of cultural heritage, and how we define autonomy in relation to craftsmanship and artistic exchange. The hand printed fabrics were then used to create parasols, a reference to the domain of tourism, oftentimes used as an outlet for commercial messages and symbols. To this day works and products from the Dutch Golden Age are still some of the most important tourist attractions in the Netherlands and form an integral part of the country's national identity."
With Niranjan Jonnalagadda and Pitchuka Srinivas

[288-318]

[288]

[290]

[291]

[292]

[293]

[289]

[294]

[295]

[296]

[297]

[298]

[299]

[300]

[301]

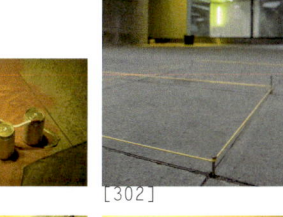
[302]

[303]

[304]

[305]

[308]

[309]

[310]

[311]

[312]

[313]

[314]

[317]

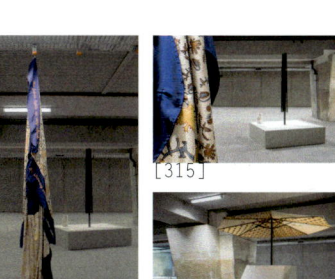
[318]

[New Town]

[319-326]
MARA
Monica Mays

"Monica Mays developed *MARA*: a performative wellness center, reality show, and office for personal and collective development. In *MARA*, leisure and labor have blended, there is no need to work for the accumulation of wealth, comfort or prestige thanks to automatization. Leisure is not mere entertainment, but an exploration of libidinal drivers.

Time is spent on developing expertise by focussing on presentness and technologies of the self in order to combat boredom and uncertainty." *Performers Alice Dos Reis, Andrea Lopez Bernal, Mathijs Walhout, Claes Storm, Sara Milio, Carl Johan Jacobsen; Sound compostion by Sun Shy Boy; Choreography by Alexey Shkolnik; Wardrobe by Paige Fruchtnicht; Graphics by Tom Kemp*

[327-329]
And Notes of, Blush-Pepper
Aaro Murphy

"For *And Notes of, Blush-Pepper*, Aaro Murphy has designed a series of fictional environments using 3D animation software. Filmed from multiple virtual camera angles, the spaces start to blur in and out of focus generating illegible revolving images. The videos are accompanied by a looping soundscape projected by series of rotary speakers, as well as a custom fragrance diffusing system. The work is part of an ongoing investigation into immersive digital culture and apparatuses of virtual architecture. By deploying high-gloss digital imagery, audio and smell, Murphy questions the tools of commercial atmospheric production and ways in which they assimilate themselves in our daily environments."
With thanks to Air Aroma.

[330-335]
Prepwork
Mirko Podkowik

"These are the three looped video channels taken from the original installation, put together into one video." *CG-Artist Sven Terhart; Sound Design by Lukas Heerich; Thanks to ZackBumm, Sonoplus, Headline Concerts and Turbinenhalle*

[336-339]
Dig: Positive Bodies
Kim Wawer

"The premise for Kim Wawer's work is the experience of embodied space. For her project *Dig*, she dug a series of holes, which were the size and scale of her body. They evoke a material intimacy and function as a breeding ground for ideas. *Dig* has resulted in sculptural earth works, in writing, and a series of concrete and latex casts. Wawer works with soil which is, like our own bodies, in an ever-changing state of flux. *Dig* approaches embodied space as an organic substance, as so called *positive bodies*. The works in the exhibition take the human scale as a basis for a series of sculpted positives. Their material gestures evoke a sense of earthly intimacy, in which form replaces the absent body."

[340-341]
Dealing with Control, A Parallel Fiction # 01
A couple driving a car along the countryside
Neeltje ten Westenend

"The profession of military policeman is permeated with layers of role-playing, which together with performance, re-enactment and fiction form the central themes of Neeltje ten Westenend's thesis research.

During her observational research in Calais, at the time of the dismantlement of the refugee camp, Ten Westenend attempted to place herself in the shoes of military policemen. Thereby she sometimes entered the role of detective, while probing into the appearances, workings and behaviour of the uniformed officers. In Amsterdam she interviewed an ex-military policeman turned actor, to get a better understanding of this double perspective. One part of the research resulted in a video work set in a military training village. *A couple driving a car along the countryside* is based on a script that in turn is based on personal experience and memory. In this experiment, which she calls a parallel fiction, Ten Westenend asked the actors to improvise on the script, emphasising the role of text and voice.

The written thesis *Dealing with Control, A Parallel Fiction* is partly a preliminary study for an essay film to deal with the double perspective within police work in which live action and role-play will alternate and sometimes overlap."

[342-345]
Boy
Kristoffer Zeiner Christiansen

"An idiosyncratic, multilayered universe was created by Kristoffer Zeiner Christiansen and situated inside the new Amsterdam Noord metro station. Experimenting with layers of virtual and fictional worlds, he created a dolphin-avatar as a representation of himself.

A character that is conceptually greater than him: more beautiful and more intelligent. Site-specific but simultaneously disconnected from its context, the work explores the possibilities of manipulation and the narrative potential of a space and objects. Inspired by his youth, he believes growing up with playing video games has changed his perception on being a young boy and being a human."

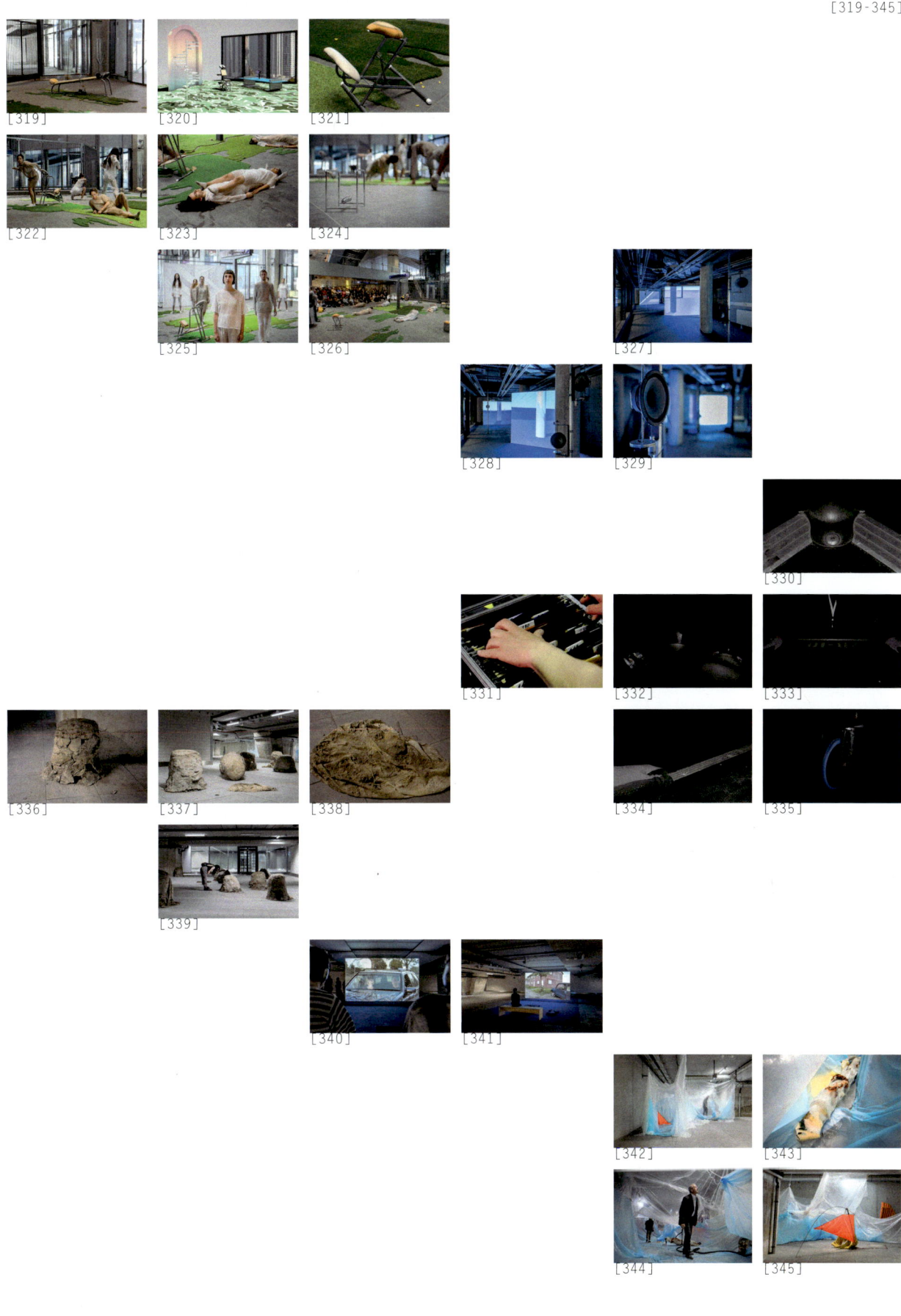

No Borders

[346-369]

Oct 2016
La Jungle
Calais FR

By *Manon Fantini, Pierre Cauderay and Leopold Banchini*
With *Lucy Stein, Colectif Perou and Silvia Converso*

"This summer, the informal settlement of Calais will reach 10'000 Inhabitants. From this point on, it will be considered a city. For more than 10 years, migrants have been living in and around Calais on their way to the UK. Various camps and squats were built and destroyed over the years, around the port of the city and the entrance of the tunnel. With the opening of the Jules Ferry Centre in 2015, surrounding settlements were destroyed or evicted. Most migrants lived behind the centre, on empty land outside of the motorway ring. The non-official, but somehow tolerated *jungle*, faced a first partial eviction in September 2015, when the houses located under the motorway bridge were destroyed. In March 2016, a second large scale eviction was organised by the government, destroying two thirds of the village. The official goal of this violent operation was to reduce the number of inhabitants to 2000 by the summer. The caterpillars flattened thousands of homes, but the operation was a failure and the Jungle inhabitants are now more numerous and organized then ever. The urban and social fabric, as well as its resistance to external attacks, will be the subject of the 5 days workshop organised by the SIS. The complex spatial construction will be examined and the role of art and design in such a context will be questioned. The students will be asked to participate in the construction of this evolving city. More than helping, it will be about learning from the inhabitants and working in solidarity with a city resisting external violence and destruction. The workshop will be organised around discussions and constructions.

Understanding the social context leading to the construction of such a city is crucial to envision possible actions leading to changes. Installing the classroom of the Studio for Immediate Spaces inside the Jungle, to facilitate discussions, will be the first step to this learning experience. The exchange of knowledge with inhabitants and locally active organisations will be enhanced through daily debate. External guests will also be brought in to the city to talk about their own practice. The citizens of the nearby city of Calais will also be invited to join. We are bringing the debate to the Jungle."

One to One

[370-386]

Feb 2019
Amsterdam NL

With *Marina Otero Verzier*

"'The narrative and data that makes inequality intelligible are made tangible through architecture.' *Jacob Moore and Susanne Schindler*

Can the construction process of a space be the project in itself? And how can it influence the resulting architecture? The economy and the politics of construction shape our built environment. The craftsmanship and the technologies set the limit of our imagination. As space designers, we think and plan the project but are often too remote from the act of construction to fully grasp it. Engaging in this process and understanding its social implication is not only empowering, but it is also a political position toward the development of our urban landscape. Reducing the critical distance separating the thoughts from the new horizons, requestioning the nature of city developments and chain of production."

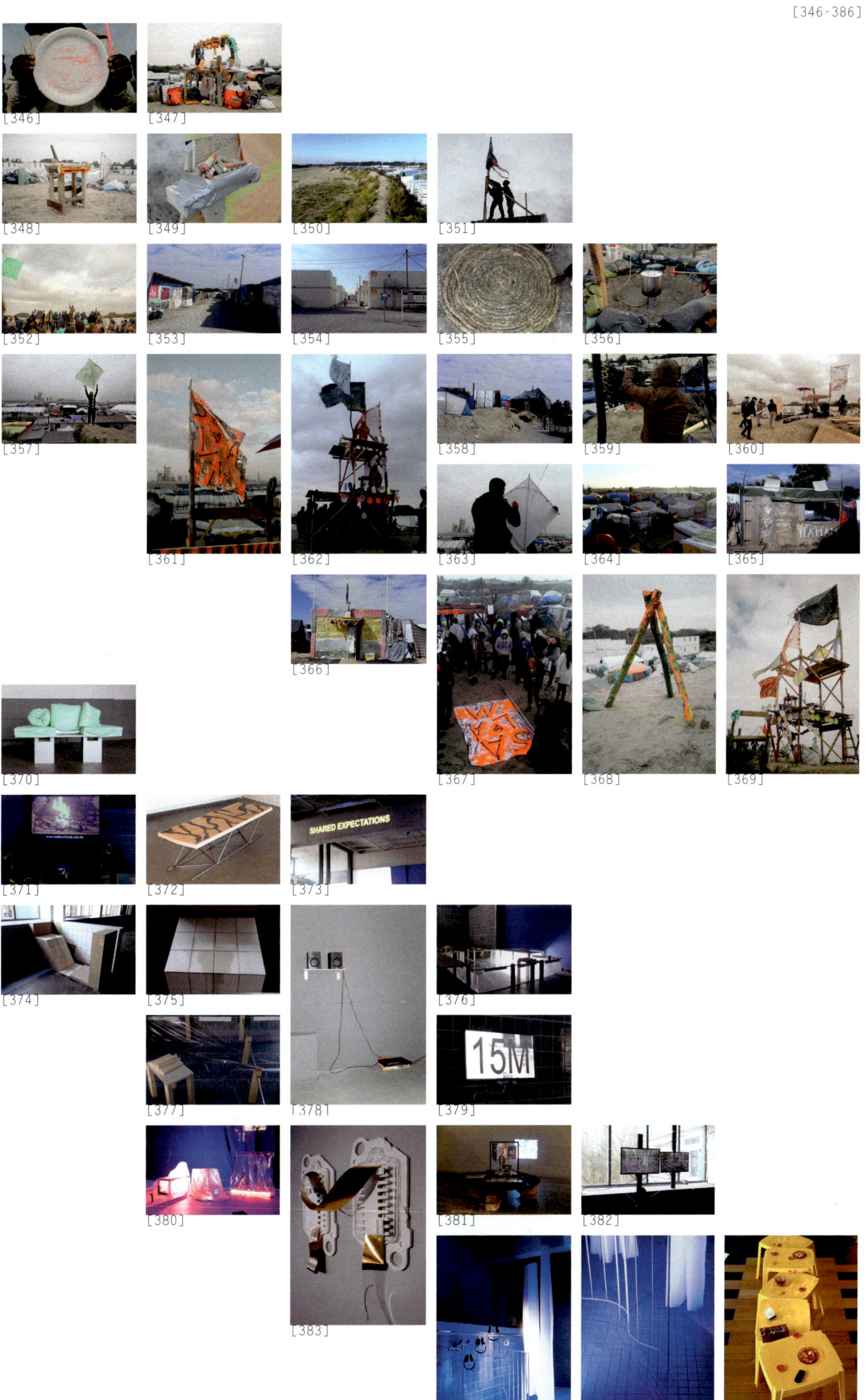

ⓔ Open Days

[387-391]   Feb 2018
[392-404]   Feb 2019

Sandberg Instituut
Amsterdam NL

"During Open Sandberg day, the public, professionals and press are invited to visit the Main Departments, Temporary Programmes and Hosted Programme at the Sandberg Instituut. A schedule with tours, special events and performances will be announced below."

ⓦ PAF

[405-413]

Feb 2019
Performing Arts Forum
St.Erme FR

By   *Andrea Zavala and Jija Sohn*
With   *School of New Dance Development, Maciek Sado and Estéfano Romani*

"The workshop will take place on a series of proposals for the entire group to engage on long durations of time. The proposals are setting up a situation in which the participants receive the instructions and engage altogether on a quest for an inmediate shift of the space, and an inmediate role in which the social and the artistic mind playfully composes the interactions. This idea comes from the desire to expand the notion of community and ethics into the artistic domain, at the same time as questioning the common rules for socialness — can they dissolve into a contemplation of landscapes and waves of consciousness? The consciousness is put at the service of the group which is put at the service of the larger picture created in time.

One of the main focus is to place the body together with its environment in constant affirmation and re-generation. Meaning that each body gains agency as it vibrates in its relation to the other bodies and objects in space. Each body is taken as an object and each object is taken as a body. Seeming the whole space from its macro-structural to its micro-structural potential, we zoom in and out, the perception of the space in minuscule and monumental fragments of scale.

We will engage also on the manufacturing, invention, transgression of the rules and parameters, as well as conversations on what is happening and how is it happening. However, the critical and theoretical dialogue will be placed inside the practice of the proposal rather than as feedback sessions."

ⓦ Palermo Appendix

[414-423]

Oct 2018
Manifesta
Palermo IT

By   *Matilde Cassani*
With   *Rotor and Ippolito Pestellini Laparelli*

"Manifesta opened its 12th edition with an alternative approach to its context, the city of Palermo. Blurring the boundaries between spaces and artworks, Palermo was positioned as the protagonist of the nomadic art biennial.

Instead of producing the usual catalogue of artistic works, an intense study of Palermo was undertaken, forming the Palermo Atlas. The Atlas became the foundation for the development of Manifesta. Offering a collection of stories on the city, it provided a preparation tool for the artists to develop their works and a medium for the visitors to establish a more meaningful connection to the surroundings. It was also expressed by Manifesta that the Atlas is their gift to the city.

Visiting the biennial we experienced the exhibition as a dialogue between the selected venues and the rest of the urban fabric. We considered Palermo as a work of art in itself, trying to expand the understanding of social capital that the Atlas suggested. We also reflected on the consequences of such an event and the potential futures for Palermo.

The appendix gathers a series of personal reflections, hypotheses, interventions, analyses and insights into the further development of the Atlas. It has been initiated by the participants of the Studio for Immediate Spaces."

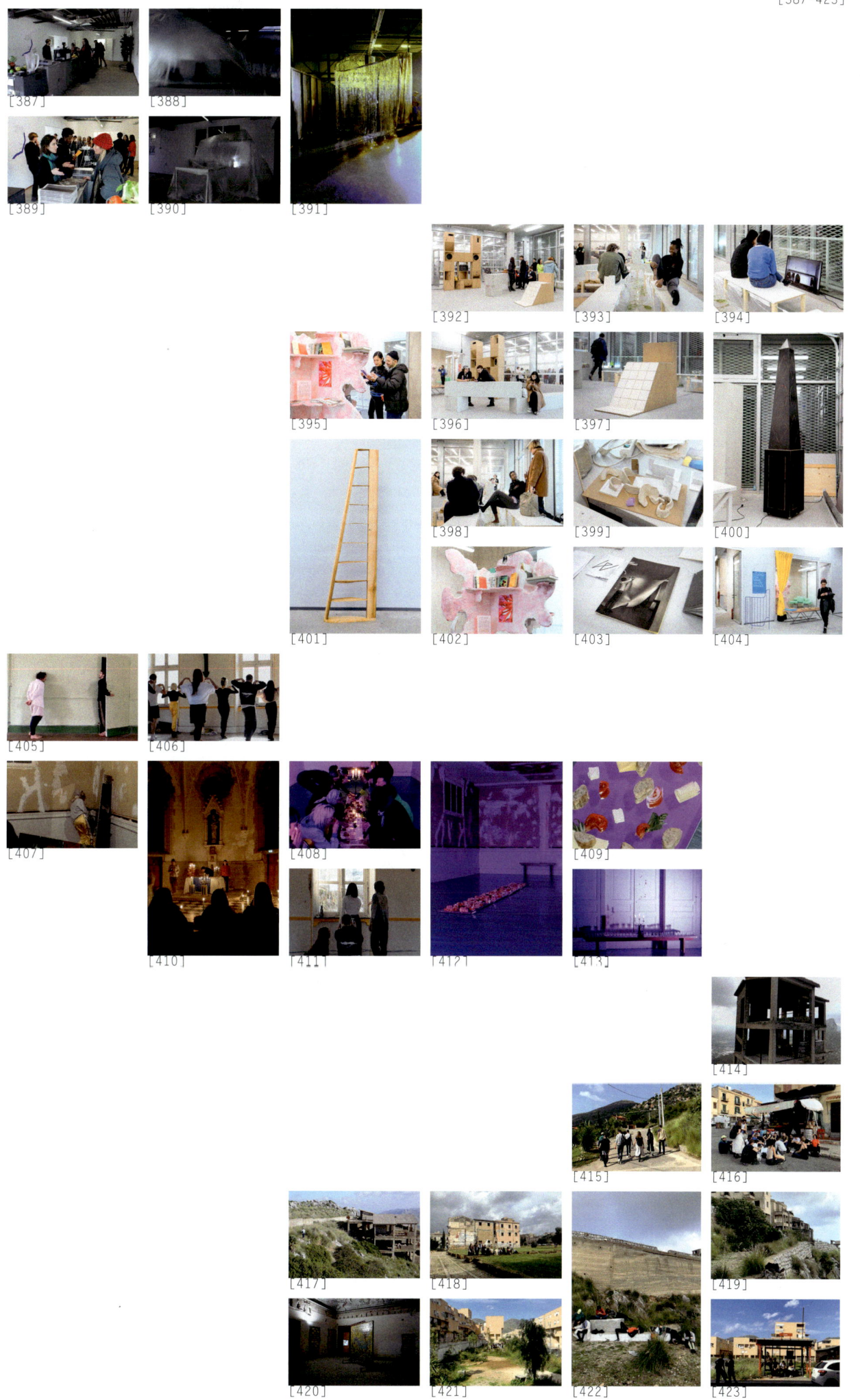

ⓔ PIC NIC

[424-427]

Jan 2019
Fabulous Future
Amsterdam NL

"Studio for Immediate Spaces *PIC NIC* invites Fabulous Future, Arie de Fijter and Kim Wawer, to present their work from during and after being in the department, what they are up to now and how the transition was after graduation. *PIC NIC* is an extravagant dinner to share and debate."

ⓢ Pick-Up

[428-434]

May 2019
Butchers Tears
Amsterdam NL

With   *Mark Redele and Femke Dekker*

"The pick-up truck is one of the key tools of today's builder. Its versatility and adaptability make it an open platform for many possible uses. It is a moving stage cruising the city unnoticed. Could it be the exhibition location of an art show?

Pick-Up is 9 public interventions on the back of a small van, brought to you on 1 screen at Butchers Tears on the 29th of May."

ⓦ Places of Production

[435-443]

Nov 2018
NL, BE

By   *Arie de Fijter and Remco Siebring*
With   *Royal Leerdam Crystal, EKWC Oisterwijk, Emaillerie Belge, School For Hand Painted Material Imitation – Van der Kelen, Royal Museum of Art and History and Kunstgieterij De Clercq-Ginsberg*

"We work with material to construct our work. How we make things depends largely on the materials we produce for our constructions. How and in which size the wood is cut influences the way we make our window frames or a wooden floor. If we openly looked at the source of the material and its production we could see the gestures we recognise in them as the start of a renewed approach. These gestures could redefine ways of making and constructing: what are the gestures that give shape to the environments we inhabit? What is the correlation between material and craft? What places of production do we see now, in the past and in the future? Seeing the past in the present, when houses were made out of mud on which the houses stood, or the temples that were carved out of the mountains."

ⓦ Port Nord

[444-453]

Oct 2017
Port Nord
Chalon-sur-Saône FR

By   *Cécile Brouse, Margaux Amoros, Pierre Cauderay and Leopold Banchini*
With   *Nelson Schaer, Xavier Juillot and La Méandre*

"*Port Nord* is a space of artistic and urban experimentation on the 1:1 scale. The project initiated in 2003 by artist and architect Xavier Juillot is dedicated to the rehabilitation of the abandoned industrial fluvial port of Chalon-sur-Saône. This research laboratory develops conceptual approaches connected with a long term practice of the site, its scales and possible reactivation.

The workshop will happen at this year's kick-off week, focussing on real-time scenography, setting up a dialogue among architectural practice and dance and transforming the industrial landscape into an endless performance. Extending the concept of performance to quotidian actions, participants will conceive scenographies for three different moments: dancing, eating and sleeping. Throughout the week, the work will develop with the aim of sharpening the ability to instantly make choices in terms of materials, lights, sounds, ingredients, locations, movements, interventions. Together with invited dancers, musicians and artists, the scenographers will be constantly challenged to increase their spontaneous abilities in order to instantly participate in the creation of situations."

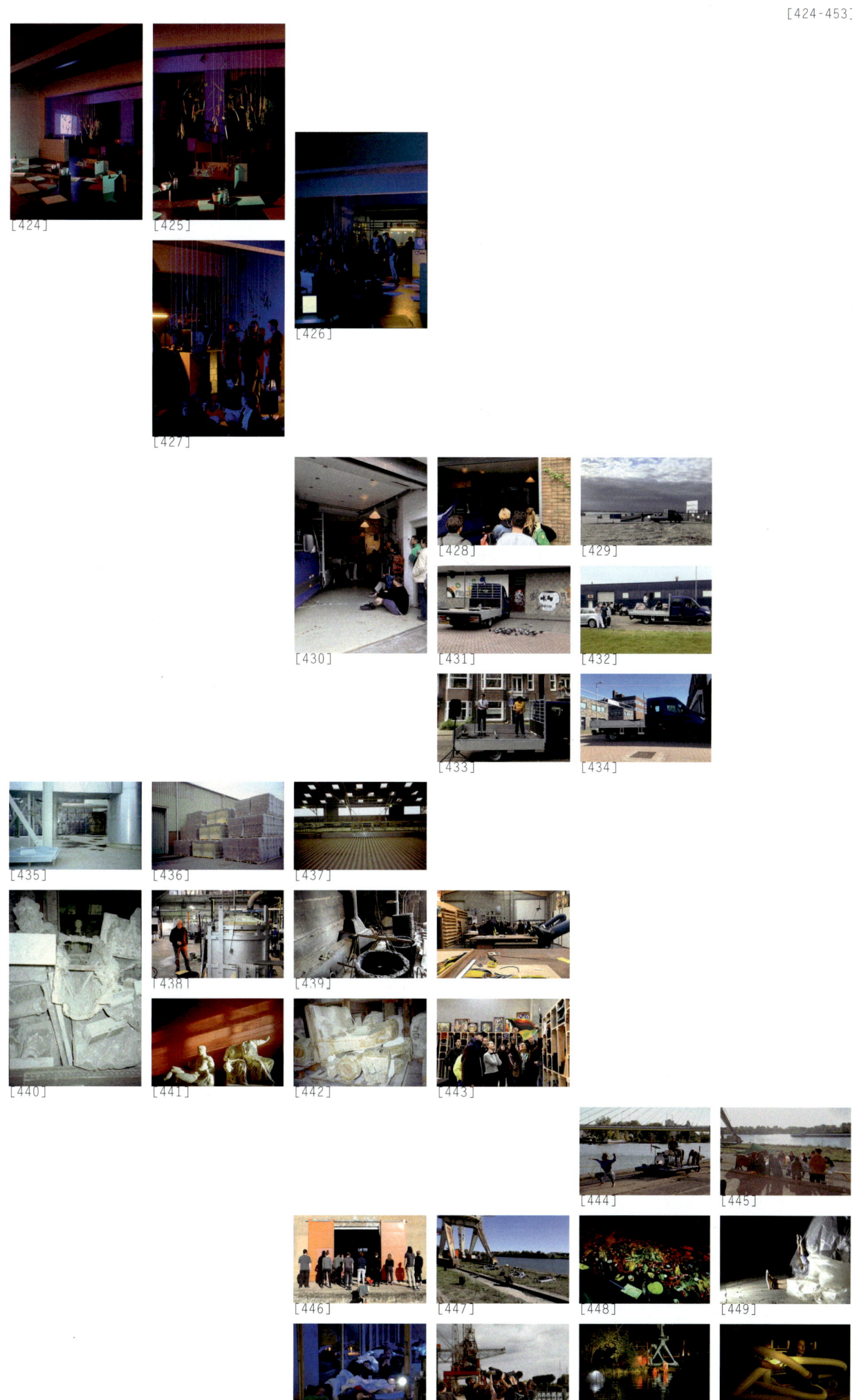

ⓦ Reclaim after Reclaim

[454-480]

Jan 2017
Manama BH

By   *Noura Al Sayeh and Anne Holtrop*
With   *Ali Alshehabi and Batool Alshaikh*

"The much-publicised urban transformations of the Gulf region have been radical in their reshaping of the urban form. Nowhere is it more apparent than along the coastline, where 80 years of cumulative land reclamation in the Kingdom of Bahrain has significantly transformed the relation to the sea. An island nation once completely dependent on the sea, through its fishing and pearling activities, has today nearly turned its back to it. Nearly, albeit for the highrises competing for a postcard view of the sea and a few disseminated fishermen's huts searching for a slice of sea along the temporary coastline.

Reclaim is an investigation into the socio-political changes that have led to the current state of affairs in view of stimulating a debate on future planning policies. The geographical retracing of national boundaries has been accompanied by a more profound social transformation — a decline of sea culture in favor of a more generic urban lifestyle. Beyond the ecological impact of land reclamation, it is an investigation into the social implications resulting in the value given to the coast as a public space.

Three fishermen's huts removed from their original sites in Bahrain form the focal point of the exhibition. The awkwardness of their situation, disconnected from their coastal scenery, relates to the discomfort of our current relation, vis a vis the coastline. This architecture without architects, through the immediacy of its architectural form, speaks of the quest for a more direct relation to the sea.

In the 1920s, similar informal coastal structures, el door, were the gathering places of pearl divers hosting the first organized syndicates. Today, scattered here and there, at the edge of the reclaimed and soon to be claimed sea, the huts host five o'clock tea sessions and backgammon games; a small attempt to reclaim a zest of leisurely coastal space."

Ⓢ Salsa

[481-492]

Jun 2017
Paleis van Mieris
Amsterdam NL

With   *Andrea Rodriguez Novoa and Joel Vacheron*

"At the end of the year, first-year participants are asked to organize an end of the year show/exhibition to showcase a completed work or research resulting from their first-year studies. This year's participants self-organized their exhibition Salsa which was located at Paleis van Mieris in Amsterdam. The show included works ranging from formal installations and performative works to multimedia investigations such as video, sound and interactive situations."

ⓦ Self Built Universes

[493-508]

May 2018
Lisbon PT

By   *Monica de Miranda*
With   *Hangar, Bruno Leitao, Hector Zamora, António Brito Guterres,*
         Carlos Carneiro, Colectivo Warehouse and Artéria

"*Military Road* (Paul Goodwin and Monica de Miranda) is a video tracing the path of a road surrounding Lisbon. The remains of this 45 km long road has now been occupied by makeshift homes built by recent immigrants. Thus, the area is considered the city's ghetto. Historically the army used the road to protect against English and French invaders — today it still acts as a fortress against *invading foreigners*, keeping immigrant populations on the margins. Developed collaboratively with local communities, *Military Road* is a reminder of how cities function and continue to function in their engagement with immigrant populations. The work highlights the impact of globalisation in the creation of multi-directional migrations of people, cultures and ideas. Impacting on geographic and cultural transformations in the spatial organisation of the world and the city, from a place of localities into a space of flux and multiple movements of people.

The workshop will deal with notions of space and territory and looks at self-built neighbourhoods in suburban Lisbon and at the same time look at how artists internationally have been referring to these marginalised spaces to reclaim political and social voices. It will be a practical and theoretical workshop with invited curators, researchers, architects and artists."

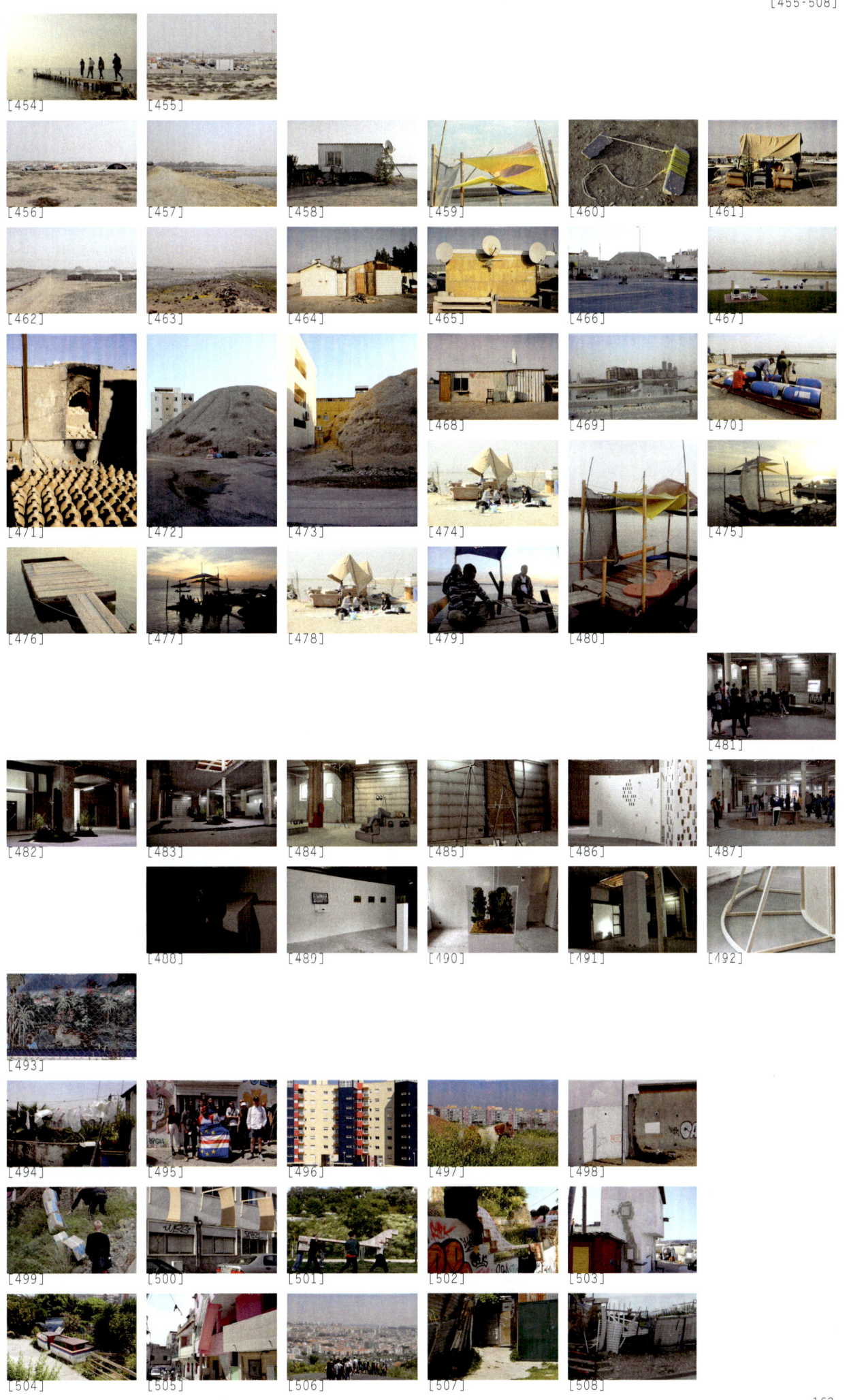

[sno-tab]

ⓦ Snow City

[509-520]

Mar 2018
Lac Lioson CH

By   *Pierre Cauderay and Louis Mejean*
With   *Gaspard Bucher, José Carron and Severain Guelpa*

"*Snow City* will take place on Lac Lioson, at 1848 meters of altitude, up in the Swiss pre-Alps. We will walk up to the frozen lake, to find a perfectly flat surface covered by snow, making it the perfect virgin field for our projects. The week will be a process of discovery, experimentation, production and a final public event. *Snow City* will be a settlement constantly developing and expanding around the jacuzzi as a central point for meetings, discussions, performances and warming. Starting from a blank *sheet*, each day infrastructure will be built by the participants developing their own means and tools of construction with snow and ice. Day by day the city will evolve and transform with the natural elements and be reshaped by the development of city traces. *Snow City* will be populated by SIS, guests and visitors, providing a unique testing ground for interactions between the studio and a public audience."

Ⓔ The Space is Closed

[521-528]

Mar 2019
Sandberg Instituut
Amsterdam NL

With   *Joseph Noonan-Ganley*

"The space is closed because
it's exhausted with customers coming without knowing what the space is about
The space is closed because
it is sick and has lost its own voice
The space is closed because
there was a lack of time to focus on its production
The space is closed because
it finds itself useless
The space is closed because
it needs to rethink the future
The space is closed because
the intended method failed to make a profit
The space is closed because
necessities were not taken into account
The space is closed because
too much was invested to recover from the crisis
The space is closed because
it doesn't understand its own name"

ⓦ The Suburban Voyage

[529-537]

Oct 2018
Rotterdam NL

By   *Leopold Banchini*
With   *Atelier Van Lieshout*

"*The Suburban Voyage* will take us through the urbanised landscapes of Holland. Reaching Amsterdam on foot from Rotterdam, we will avoid the picturesque and tourist centers to focus on the inbetween. Our safari will be self-suffient and each day we will create the necessary commodities of our survival. Using the model of the *cadavre exquis*, each day will be carefully organised by a group in secret. Each group will have to prepare the route, build a shelter and cook food for a specific day. Each shelter (tent, inflatable, cave ...) will be built on location and will include a specific DIY kitchen for one night. The travel agency van will carry the heavy materials for us and each group will be allocated storage of one cubic meter of material in it. Each participant should bring a good sleeping bag, a camping mattress as well as good shoes, warm and rainproof clothes. Our meeting point will be in Rotterdam on the 30th of September in the evening and we shall reach the Sandberg Institute on Friday afternoon."

ⓦ Table of Content

[538-541]

Apr 2019
De Fabriek
Eindhoven NL

By   *Ludovic Balland, Julius Betke and Marlow Peplow*
With   *Academy of Fine Arts Leipzig*

"Measuring the archive — Atlas of SIS
Imagine an archive as a physical space. Is it just a passive storage, containing images and texts, or could it be an active generator for future creations?

The purpose of the workshop in Eindhoven is to create a mapping of the archive of the Studio for Immediate Spaces. This mapping depends on parameters, which you will develop in this time. Think about a categorisation to find links between the methodology weeks which have taken place in the past and will take place in the future.

Depending on your individual practice, the form of reflection and reconstruction of the current archive is up to you as long as the outcome can be used as a parameter for the mapping.

Students of Hochschule für Grafik und Buchkunst will set up a Live-Desktop-Publishing environment to create a graphical map based upon your parameters. This outcome will be used as a key concept for the upcoming catalogue of Studio for Immediate Spaces."

[509-541]

[509]

[510]

[511]

[512]

[513]

[514]

[515]

[516]

[517]

[518]

[519]

[520]

[521]

[522] [523] [524]

[525]

[526]

[527]

[528]

[529]

[530]

[531]

[532]

[533]

[534]

[535]

[536] [537]

[538]

[539]

[540]

[541]

ⓢ Tabula Rasa

[542-566]

Dec 2018
Amsterdam NL

With *Arna Mackic and Boris de Beijer*

"'The destructive character knows only one watchword, make room and only one activity: clearing away. It clears away the traces of our own age and has few needs, and the least of them is to know what will replace what has been destroyed.' *Walter Benjamin*

The *Tabula Rasa*, as a desire for sweeping away the past and creating a potential site for the construction of utopian dreams, it is one of the obsessions of Modernist Architecture. Stating the utopia can be created on the existing bases of the past. The show introduces the works into the pre-existing urban fabric and confronts them to an unselected audience."

ⓦ Testing the Frontline

[567-574]

Dec 2017
Nieuw West,
The Bijlmer and Vogelbuurt
Amsterdam NL

By *Roel Griffioen and Rosa te Velde*
With *Miguel Heilbron, Amy Abdou, Tessa Hendriks and Kees Visser*

"During this methodology week, we will explore the manifestations and politics of gentrification in the city of Amsterdam. Together with Roel Griffioen we will discuss, analyse, problematise and intervene in the so-called *frontline* of gentrification in the city of Amsterdam.

Gentrification is often packaged and promoted as *revitalisation*, *neighbourhood improvement* or *community transformation*, but should be understood as a spatialised battle over the right to the city: who belongs in the city, and to whom does the city belong? Artists and *creative producers* are implicated in these processes in various and complex ways, often without them being conscious of them.

What is gentrification, and how does it manifest itself? What are the trajectories and histories of gentrification? What is the language of gentrification? How are racial and economic segregations related to this process? What are the aesthetics of gentrification? What are its visual and spatial precedents? How does the built environment (both inside and outside) facilitate and attract, include and exclude specific groups of people? What are the specificities of the design, interior design, the architecture and the urban fabric that influence the mechanisms of separation? And what could be effective tactics or strategies to oppose these processes?

During this weeklong course we will critically explore terminologies, histories, and theories of gentrification, while also practically engaging in the current gentrification battlefields within the city. Lectures, presentations, and film screenings will be combined with walks through different Amsterdam neighbourhoods and hands-on fieldwork."

ⓦ Una Visita Guiada

[575-587]

Mar 2018
De Fabriek
Eindhoven NL

By *Jordi Colomer and Andrea Rodriguez Novoa*

"Space Readers? Reading the space?

Join at 5–8pm on the 30th March 2018 for a public guided tour in the city of Eindhoven. A choral reading of what a city could be will be presented through time, space, experience and storytelling as a collective output from the week-long workshop, *Una visita guiada*. Starting point De Fabriek Eindhoven.

This tour is the result of a weeklong workshop at De Fabriek, asking the question of how to build space by means of writing and reading it.

During the week, the group got lost in an unknown city, walked together through and along different spaces, made new plans of the city and had hot discussions about what a city is, in order to build up their own guided visit. We want to explore re-appropiation of a local, global, changing and multiple-languaged space, as a critical, politicised look to the land.

A one-week workshop with tutors Jordi Colomer and Andrea Rodriguez Novoa on how to build space by means of writing and reading it.

We will walk together through and along different spaces and visit diverse spots in the city of Eindhoven. A tour driven by the tutors with the help of local practitioners of (un)related fields whose eyes and words will be the starting point to re-imagine those sites and for the participants to build up their own guided visit of the town and its outskirts. We would like them to read this exercise as a re-appropiation of a local, global, changing and multiple-languaged space, as a critical, politicized look to the land, that they are going to share in a final public guided visit."

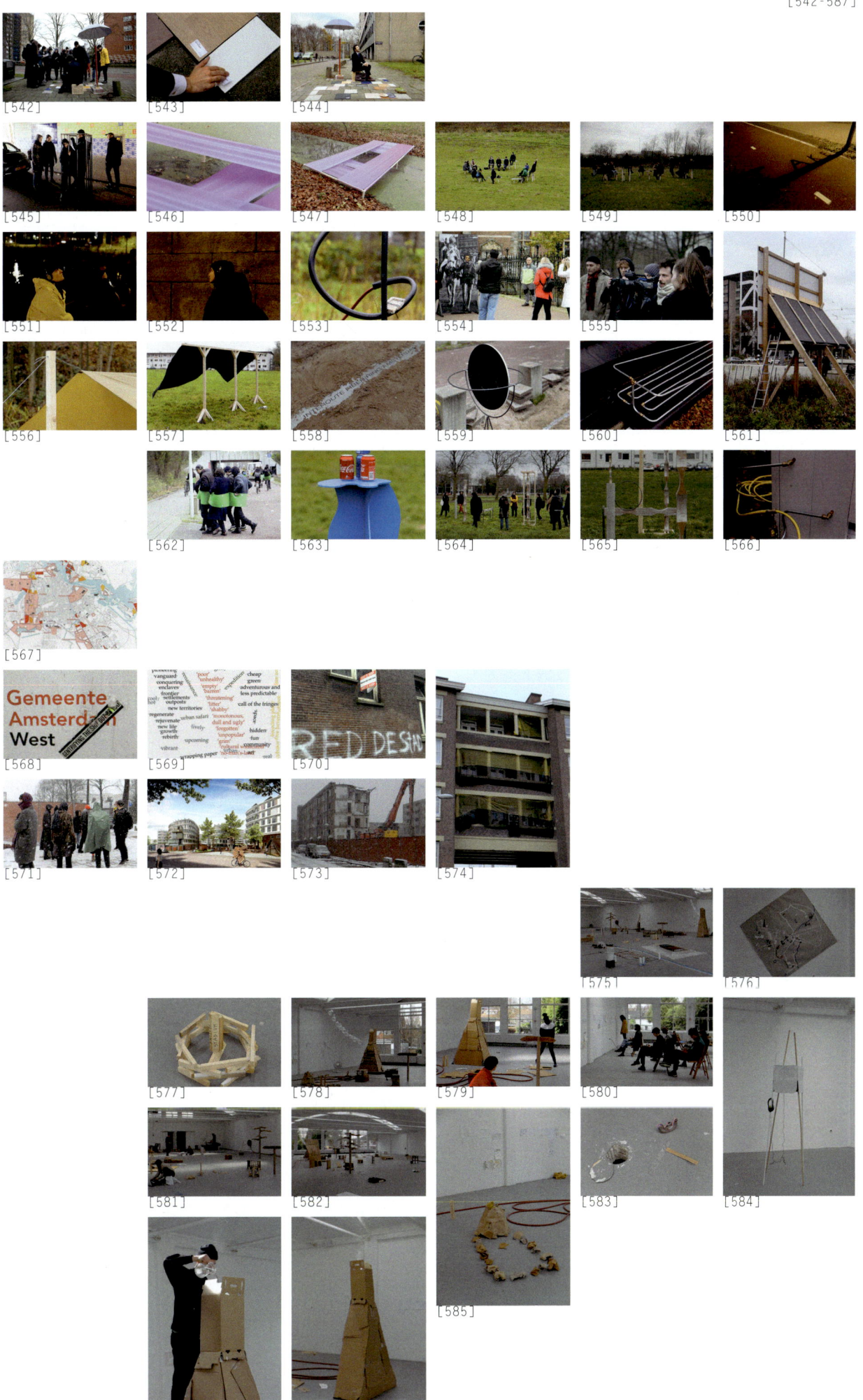

[une-zoo]

Unequal Club

[588-599]

Jan 2018
DeSchool Club
Amsterdam NL

By *Amal Alhaag and Maria Guggenbichler*

"The *Unequal Club* is a social situation.

The *Unequal Club* does not provide the innocence of, nor the temporary escape from inequality, exclusion, misery, oppression, alienation or sadness. It keeps them at sight. It includes them. It keeps them loose, it keeps them close to the chest. The *Unequal Club* senses discomfort, together with others. It is a depressed gathering, a difficult conversation, a short-distance conflict.

The *Unequal Club* re-claims the club as a place of queer histories and gatherings; for sexual, social and political education and organising. It is an archive for queer community, support, survival and mourning. "The contexts from which the Deep House sound emerged are forgotten: sexual and gender crises, transgendered sex work, black market hormones, drug and alcohol addiction, loneliness, racism, HIV, ACT- UP, Thompkins Sq. Park, police brutality, queer-bashing, underpayment, unemployment and censorship — all at 120 beats per minute. House wasn't so much a sound as a situation." DJ Sprinkles
Without inequality no need for a border. No nation state without border.
Without a border no smuggling.
No bribing without authorities.
If you are somebody, the *Unequal Club* is not for you. The *Unequal Club* is for nobodies (Nobodies- against-the-state).
Do you have any advice for white activist allies? — Get out the way.
The *Unequal Club* is a labyrinth of closing doors, shape shifting, scamming and failing interactions. This club sweats, shakes, stammers, sometimes dances, sometimes passes out to the rhythms of access and exclusion. It is the homestead where bouncers, alienation, up rootedness, obstacles, smuggle, theft, passing, getting out of the way and way making forms its world-making.
Why do I need I.D. to get I.D.? (I don't know, beats me ... beats me) If I had I.D. I wouldn't need I.D.
Fake I.Ds. Fake identities. Trade names. Bribe the bouncer. Distract the door bitch. Scam the system. Mess up the boundaries. Everyone is on the guest list, but do you know who you are?"

The Wild Beyond

[600-603]

April 2017
Amsterdam NL

By *Dorine van Meel*
With *Sibiya Simangaliso*

"We cannot say that new structures will replace the ones we live with yet, because once we have torn this shit down, we will inevitably see more and see differently and feel a new sense of wanting and being and becoming. What we want after "the break" will be different from what we think we want before the break and both are necessarily different from the desire that issues from being in the break. *Jack Halberstam* in *"The Wild Beyond: With and for the Undercommons"*

In this week-long workshop we will explore the notion of the *wild beyond* as proposed by Harney and Moten in their book The Undercommons from 2013. Their call to collectively enter this wild space, where disorder rules, starts from the acknowledgement that we live in a broken world that goes beyond repair. Through a number of (writing) assignments and discussions we will join in their endeavour to "take apart, dismantle, tear down the structure that, right now, limits our ability to find each other, to see beyond it and to access the places that we know lie outside its walls." We will work towards the development of a spatial installation in which we will present our collective efforts to imagine and stage The Wild Beyond to an audience at the end of the week."

Zoomscape

[604-626]

Dec 2018
Fabulous Future
Amsterdam NL

By *Sofia Mourato and The One Minute Foundation*
With *Neeltje Ten Westenend*

"*Zoomscape* aims to explore the impact of the moving image when representing space. By camera reproduction the perception of architecture spaces seen in motion, break apart, and recombine. Attentiveness to space depends upon the context of the experience. When connected to art (as in a museum exhibition), to collective history (the site of a famous event), to personal history (someone's childhood home or neighbourhood), to celebrity (the home of a politician or film star), or to a media story (the design competition of the WTC), spaces acquire a larger meaning. Like most things, spaces mean more when they mediate the extraordinary moments of life.

Bringing together the workshop participants, a curator and a specialized technical team, along with three artists talks, a short films programme and a final presentation of the works, *Zoomscape* workshop aims to unveil that different people can "zoom" into a space using several modes of experience, resulting in a reframing within today's predominantly visual culture.

The workshop will be held in a building awaiting a scheduled demolition, an old school built in the 60's that is now the last standing proof of what once was the surrounding area. Expensive luxury apartments and many hotels including the newest OMA project for a hotel now surround the building."

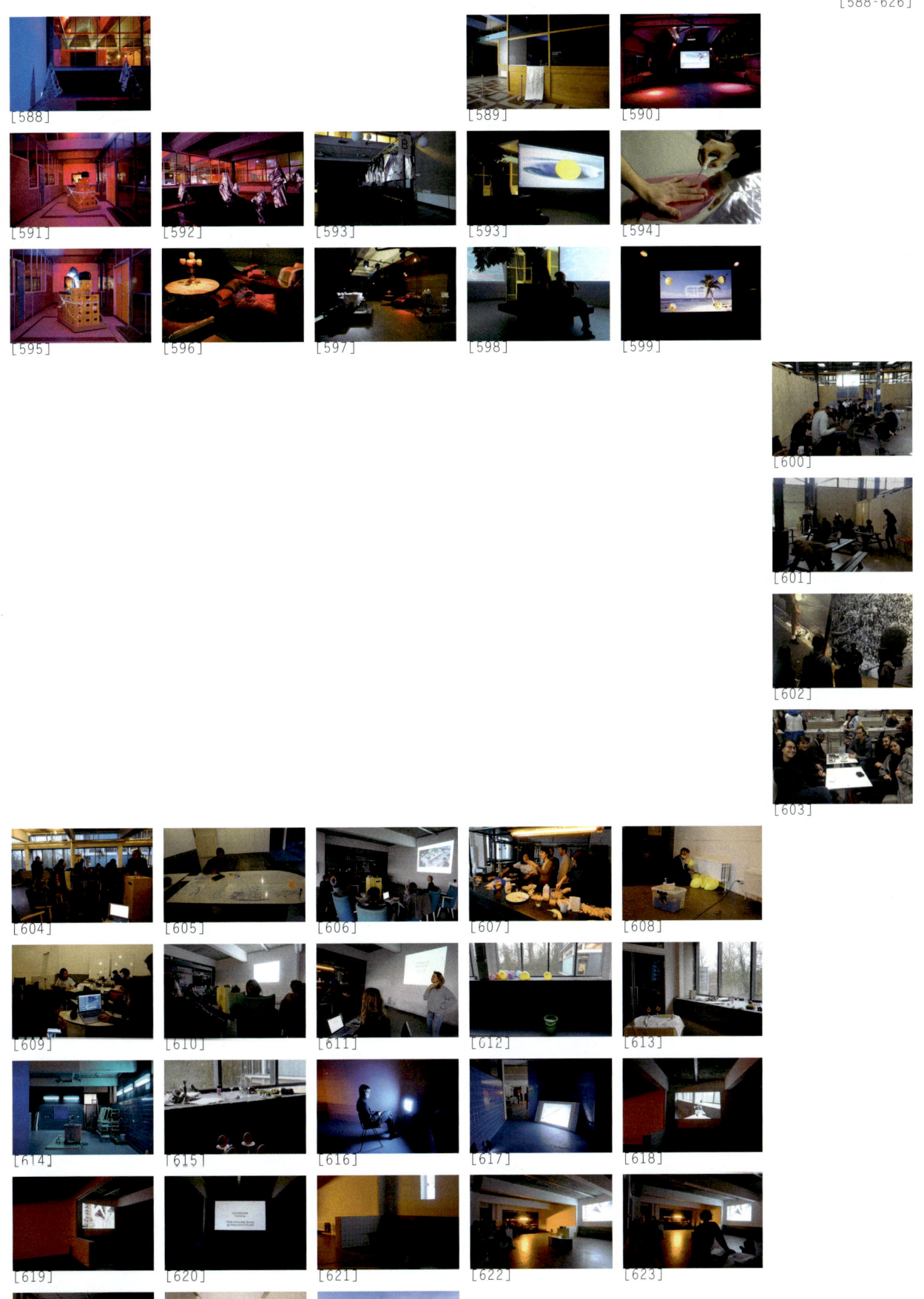

[Colophon]

- **Studio for Immediate Spaces**
  Director 2016 – 2019: Leopold Banchini

- **Tutors 2016 – 2019**
  Arie de Fijter
  Elise Van Mourik
  Hélène Webers
  Joseph Noonan-Ganley
  Julian Schubert
  Laure Jaffuel
  Leopold Banchini
  Marie-Avril Berthet
  Matilde Cassani
  Remco Siebring
  Rosa te Velde
  Tom Vandeputte

- **Guests 2016 – 2019**
  Academy of Fine Arts Leipzig
  Ali Al Shehabi
  Amal Alhaag
  Amelia Groom
  Amy Abdou
  Andrea Rodriguez Novoa
  Andrea Zavala
  Andy Vidal
  Anne Dessing
  Anne Holtrop
  António Brito Guterres
  Arna Mačkić
  Artéria
  Atelier Van Lieshout
  Aurélien Lepetit
  Bas Hendrix
  Batool Alshaikh
  Bitnik Mediengruppe
  Boris de Beijer
  Bruno Leitão
  Carlos Carneiro
  Cécile Brouse
  Céline Talens
  Christine Roggeman
  Claire Potter
  Clément Carat
  Colectif Perou
  Colectivo Warehouse
  Daniel Zamarbide
  De Fabriek Volkskamer
  Délage and the Togetherness
  Dieter Dietz
  Dorine van Meel
  Estéfano Romani
  Esther Genicot
  Fabulous Future
  Femke Dekker
  Femke Herregraven
  Finder of Things
  Fran Edgerley
  Frédéric Post
  Gaspard Bucher
  Gieneke Pieterse
  Héctor Zamora
  Ibo Ventura & Gaby Vineyard
  Ignas van Rijckevorsel
  Ippolito Pestellini Laparelli
  Ivan Cheng
  Jerszy Seymour
  Jesse James
  Jija Sohn
  João Rebelo Costa
  Joël Vacheron
  Jordi Colomer
  Josè Carron
  Jurgen Bey
  Katinka de Jonge
  Kees de Haan
  Kim Wawer
  Krijn De Koning
  Kristoffer Zeiner Christiansen
  La Méandre
  Lara Almarcegui
  Louis Mejean
  Lucy Stein
  Ludovic Balland
  Ludwig Engel
  Luis Brum
  Lukas Feireiss
  Maciek Sado
  Madara
  Manon Fantini
  Margarita Osipian
  Margaux Amoros
  Maria Guggenbichler
  Marina Otero Verzier
  Márk Minkjan
  Mark Redele
  Matt Stokes
  Miguel Heilbron
  Mónica de Miranda
  Neelje Ten Westenend
  Nelson Schaer
  Noura Al Sayeh
  One Minute Foundation
  Orchid
  Orit Gat
  Paolo Patelli
  Paul Chatterton
  Paulien Bremmer
  Pepper Metz
  Pierre Cauderay
  Pipa Collada
  Radical Cut-Up Department
  Rainer Hehl
  Rebecca Jagoe
  Roel Griffioen
  Rotor
  Roy Claire Potter
  Samantha Thole
  School of New Dance Development
  Séverin Guelpa
  Sibiya Simangaliso
  Silvia Converso
  Simon Fujiwara
  Sofia Carolina Botelho
  Sofia Mourato
  Tessa Hendriks
  The Dirty Art Departement
  Tom Dillon
  Valentin Noiret
  Vanlentijn Byvanck
  Very High Tea
  Walk and Talk Festival
  Xavier Juillot
  Yana Foqué
  Zoltán Kisák & Dániel Meste

- **Participants 2016 / 2017**
  Aaro Murphy
  Arie de Fijter
  Carolin Gießner
  Eva Hoonhout
  Gauthier Chambry
  Giedre Lisauskaite
  Hein van Duppen
  Kim Wawer
  Kristoffer Zeiner Christiansen
  Liene Pavlovska
  Lily Lanfermeijer
  Malissa Anne Canez Sabus
  Mirko Podkowik
  Monica Mays
  Nadjim Bigou
  Naomi Credé
  Neeltje ten Westenend
  Niels Albers
  Rein Verhoef
  Samuel Kuhfuss Gustavsen
  Shih-Hui Hung
  Zsofia Szoke

- **Participants 2017 / 2018**
  Andrea Belosi
  Antoine Guay
  Davide-Christelle Sanvee
  Elia Castino
  Elizaveta Strakhova
  Maike Statz
  Mathilde Helbo Stubmark
  Stijn van Kervel

- **Participants 2018 / 2019**
  Ali Glover
  Andoni Zamora Chacartegui
  Beatriz Conefrey
  Julica Morlok
  Kyulim Kim
  María Mazzanti
  Michael Weber
  Roman Tkachenko
  Ruben Mols
  Thorben Gröbel
  Wei-Tung Kuo

- **Writers**
  Mark Minkjan
  Lukas Feireiss
  Leopold Banchini
  Marie-Avril Berthet
  Julian Schubert
  Ludwig Engel
  Fabulous Future
  Maike Statz

  If not mentioned all reprinted text are published with the kind permission of the authors and right holders

- **Photo Credits**
  Sandberg Instituut
  Sander van Wettum (DOP)
  Tom Janssen
  Willem de Kam
  Robert Glas
  Luuk Smits
  Geisje van der Linden

  For Fabulous Future
  Aad Hoogendoorn
  Francesca Luccitta

  Special thanks to all the Participants and Contributors for their Photos

[One to One Contribution by Elia Castino]

[Table of Work]

This extended appendix chapter reflects the editorial investigation we made during the workshop "Table of Content" [p164]. The Workshop displayed the visual material of the "Studio for Immediate Spaces", collected during the past three years, aimed towards the understanding of their working method and how we appropriate and edit that method. The daily investigations we made during the workshop were later used as the editorial structure of the publication.

[Mobile office installed in the cellar of "De Fabriek" in Eindhoven where the workshop "Table of Content" took place.]

● STATUS-QUO

Where are we? What is our destination offering to us? The cellar is cleared out and the page is white. We assimilate our location by measuring the space and setting up a working-enviroment. Is it our constraint to force the space into a grid or is this our method?

[The cellar was divided into 8 cells. We named these cells "editorial cells".]

[Tables of DeFabriek]

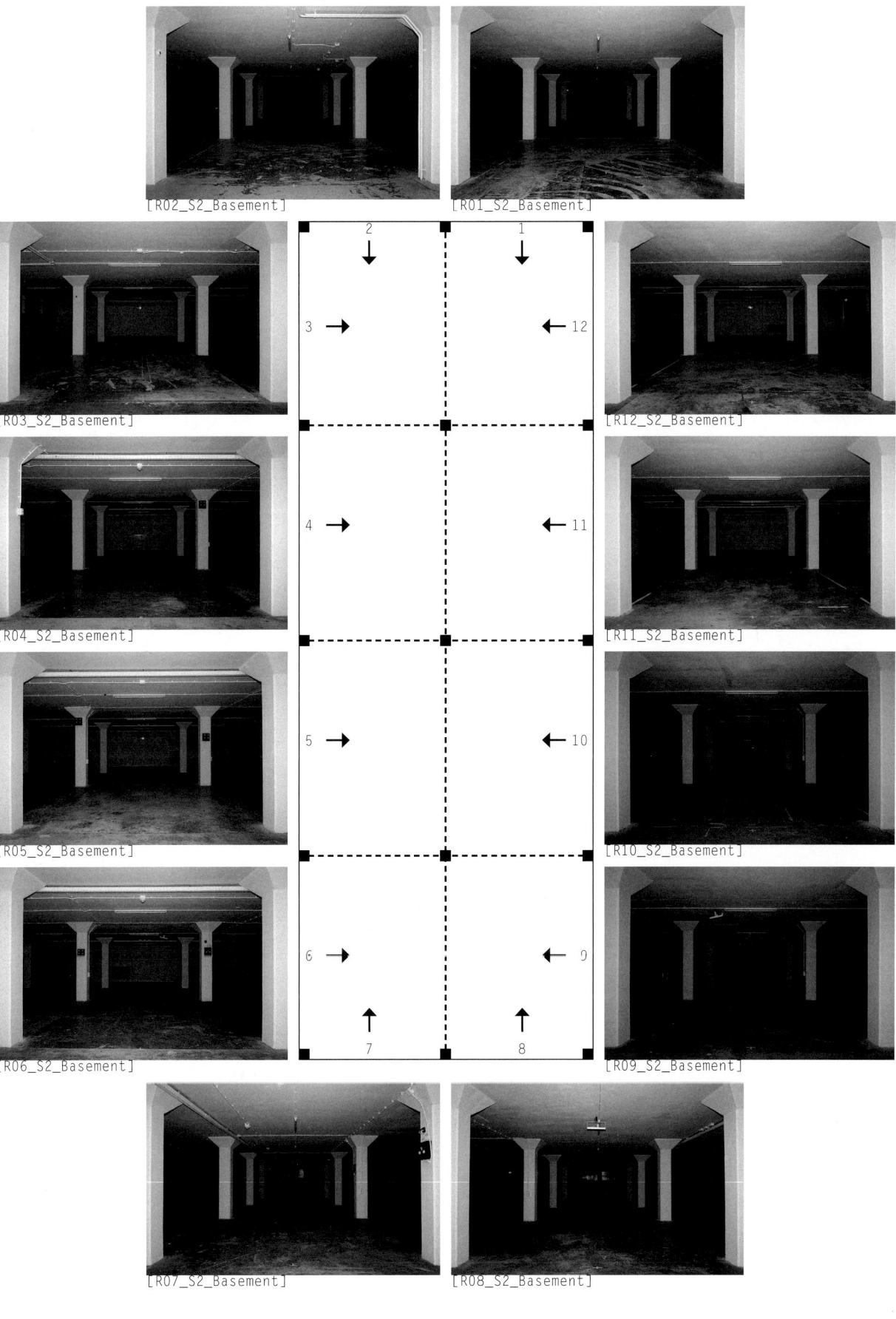

[Tables of Order]

[Various arrangements of the given index of locations and participants related to the SIS workshops were displayed inside the "editorial cells".]

●● IN-SITU

What are we doing here? What is the Studio for Immediate Spaces telling us? Who are these names and the locations? What is happening in Amsterdam and what is happening in the world? Are we talking the same language?

[Every Studio-project workshop was transformed into an abstract, small size 3-dimensional paper elevation model.] →

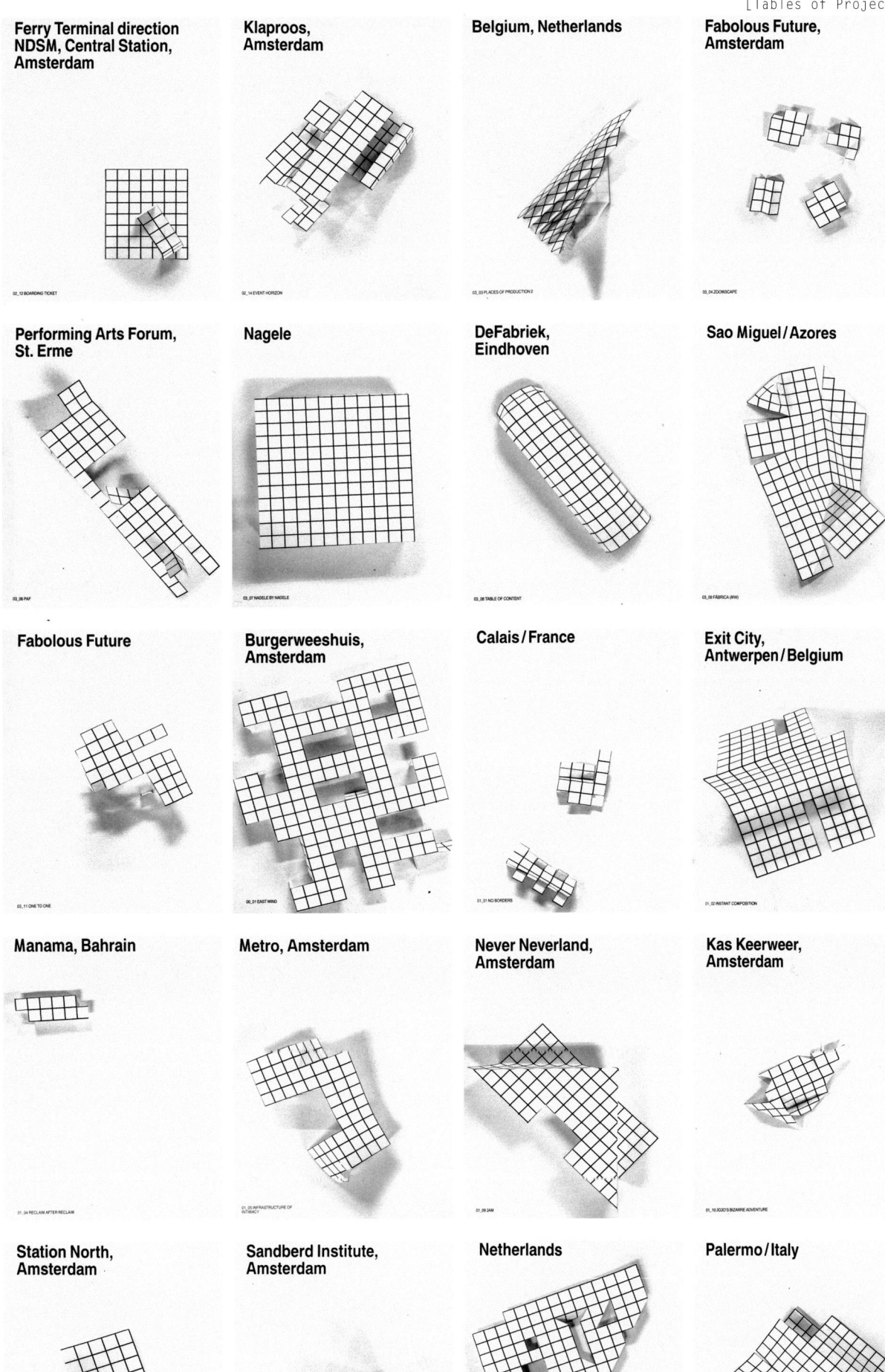

[Project Rendering]

[M10_Render_ALPHA-7_56]
[M10_Render_ALPHA-7_72]
[M10_Render_ALPHA-7_12]
[M10_Render_ALPHA-7_38]

[City of Content]

[Organization of the 3-dimensional paper elevation models as a city of content. This pseudo urbanistic arrangement aimed to discover and display new links between the different IS-project workshops.]

●●● TALK—OVER   What can we learn from architects, researchers and urban planners? Is an urban enviroment our common platform to debate about an upcoming publication? Can we build a city made out of an archive to investigate its content?

← [The 3-dimensional paper elevation models were used to build up a series of larger scale tables. These table structures were used to display and investigate the visual material of Studio.]

[Tables of Action]

[The table structures, or display structure, allowed us to layout the given visual material in a nonlinear fashion. The editorial work becomes 3-dimensional.]

●●●● BUILD-UP

Can we adapt methods from the Studio? How can we build up an editable content for the upcoming publication? Does it spread into the horizontal or more into the vertical? How does the content react in space?

[Tables of Action]

[Using the height and the depth of the cellar and editorial cells, the visual associations between each image could be observed from different angles.]

[Tables of Links]

[The given visual material itself gets transformed into objects, using several hierarchy sizes.]

●●●●● AFTERMATH

What paradigmas can we extract out of the last three years? Can the table of content be an example for the practice of the Studio for Immediate Spaces? What happens if we break it down and re-arrange the extract. Will this tell a new story?

[Tables of Links]

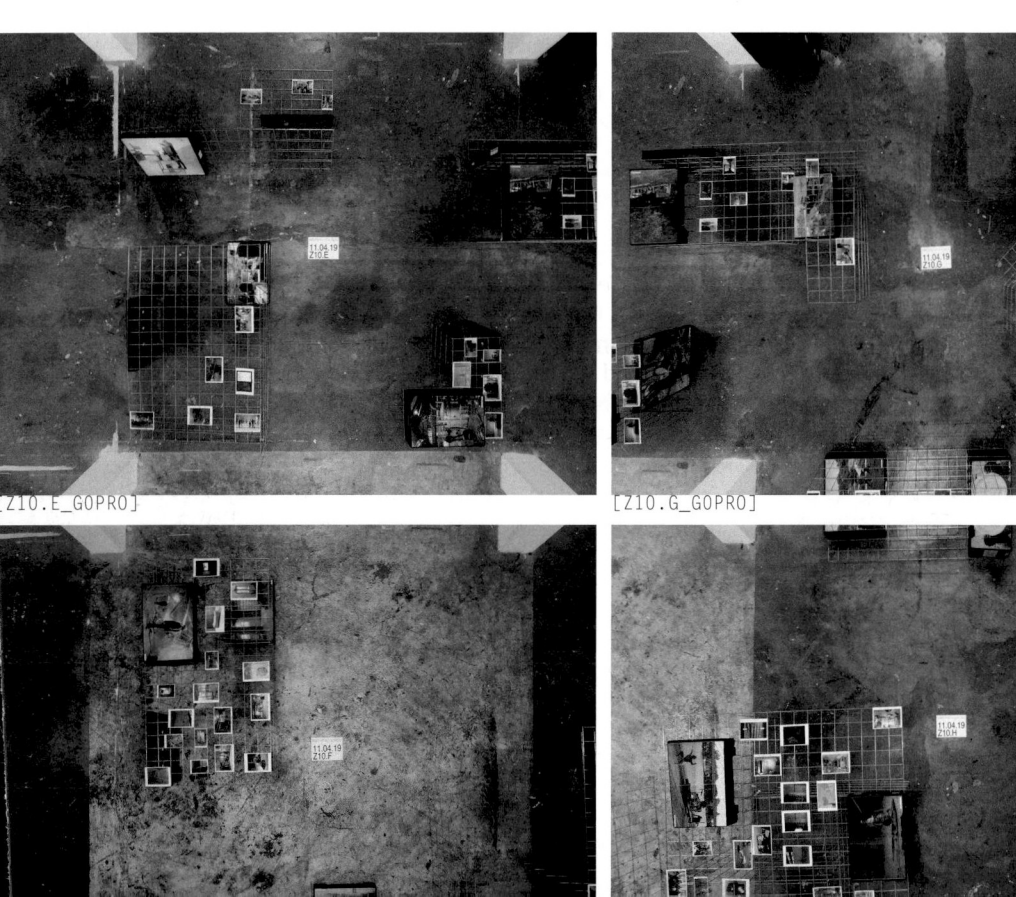

181

TYPOGRAPHIC EPILOGUE — LUDOVIC BALLAND / JULIUS BETKE / MARLOW PEPLOW-LOHMANN

Linear Editing Editing has long been a very linear job, and to a certain extent still is. The various roles involved in (predigital) book production were always very clearly defined: there was an author, a publisher, a printer and a binder. The graphic designer worked for the publisher, either in-house or independently. The publisher was responsible for content editing, copy editing and proof reading. Larger publications would often require an external editor. There was even a time when the designer, the publisher and the author could rely on the services of a type setter. The type setter would set the text at the specified size and line spacing. The type-set text was then transferred to film and exposed. These clearly defined responsibilities had to follow a certain sequence if books were to be produced and published at all. Interestingly, publishers back then seem to have produced more books more quickly than we do today.

Spatial Editing These responsibilities have now changed completely, and the production process is anything but linear. Can we speak of a spatial editing process, then, a process where the various tasks are 'stacked' and carried out simultaneously? At any rate, authors are rarely able to deliver print-ready content these days. Publishers are struggling to stay afloat, and designers are increasingly taking an editorial role. We're responsible for the format, the series, the structure and ultimately also the materiality of the publication.

Experimental Editing In producing this publication we've experimented with a completely new approach to editing. Graphic design students from the typography course at the Academy of Fine Arts Leipzig and a group of masters' students from the Sandberg Institute for the Studio of Immediate Spaces locked themselves up in a room for a week. The process of getting to know the accumulated material of more than three years of research at the Immediate Spaces Master Class was conceived spatially. The material wasn't sent via the usual WeTransfer links. It was methodically laid out, sorted, queried and analysed. In the first phase the participants drew on their memories of past projects to design abstract, intuitive paper models. In the second phase the material was sorted according to quality and translated into three-dimensional wire mesh structures. These structures were initially regarded as pure objects. The end result was a series of abstract frameworks, some large, some linear, others contorted. These structures or content containers were later used as 'tables of content'. The content itself — photographs printed at various sizes, some mounted on board – was laid out horizontally or strung up vertically according to the various organising principles of the 'tables of content'.

The room we were in — originally a bookbinder's workshop — had its own basic structure of regularly placed pillars. We referred to the subdivisions of this pre-existing structure as 'editorial cells'. These cells were used for certain sub-themes and specific editorial investigations, which were fully documented every day.

Mimetic Editing The week-long workshop generated a unique experience of the content. Besides looking at the material, the aim of the workshop was to question the approach of the Immediate Spaces studio. In the present publication this approach is subdivided into five groups:

- ● *STATUS-QUO* [current state]
- ●● *IN-SITU* [appropriation]
- ●●● *TALK-OVER* [working process]
- ●●●● *BUILD-UP* [implementation]
- ●●●●● *AFTERMATH* [end result]

We wanted to appropriate it. We wanted to avoid a linear form of editing and instead become part of the content, if only for a short time.

Mapping We've produced this publication in the form of an atlas, though there are no maps and certainly no predetermined routes. Instead we wanted the elaborate editorial structure of the book to bring out the multiple potential readings of the content. The main section of the book — *STATUS-QUO, IN-SITU, TALK-OVER, BUILD-AFTERMATH* — brings these sites together into an associative system. We chose not to reveal this structural system because we saw it as more of a skeletal structure in the background. The themes can and should only be perceived visually.

Methodologies Along with the new name of the Studio for Immediate Spaces they also elaborated a completely new method. The focus is still on architecture and interior design — the former name of the master class — but the projects are more sociological, geographical and archaeological in their approach. The aims and available means, restructuring and spatial transformations that happen within the projects are strongly bound up with local and economic factors. They're interventions. As designers we now find ourselves at the interface of responsibilities, and this affects how we handle the content we're given. The potential of the new process we've devised for this publication ultimately says something about how we see and understand content, and how we appropriate it. Publishing itself becomes a bearer of content and no longer just a service. an apparatus for deconstructing, researching and reframing content.